Evaluating Character Development

51 Tools for Measuring Success

EDWARD F. DeROCHE, Ph.D.

Director, International Center for Character Education
Professor, School of Education, University of San Diego

Evaluating Character Development: 51 Tools for Measuring Success

Publisher: Character Development Group, Inc.
P.O. Box 9211, Chapel Hill, NC 27515-9211
919.967.2110, Fax: 919.967.2139
E-mail: info@CharacterEducation.com
www.CharacterEducation.com

Text editing by Ginny Turner
Cover and text design by Sara Sanders

ISBN: 1-892056-40-2

$39.95

Printed in the United States of America

Acknowledgments

Few authors write a book alone. There are those that contribute to an author's ideas. There are those that help the author find time to write. There are those who provide encouragement when the author's enthusiasm begins to wane. There are those who read the manuscript over and over finding typos, seeking clarity, and offering advice and suggestions about content and format. Then there are those that do the final editing and design the book to make it attractive to the reader.

My thanks and appreciation to:

Jacqueline, my wife, who arranges the time, provides the encouragement!

Dr. Mary Williams, my colleague in character education who willingly shares her knowledge and skills!

C.J. Moloney and other specialists in character education for reading the manuscript and trying out some of the instruments in their schools and classrooms!

Ginny Turner, who exemplifies my view that every author needs a good editor!

Sara Sanders for her attractive cover and book design work!

About the Author

Edward DeRoche, Ph.D., has had a variety of educational experiences ranging from elementary and middle school teacher and principal, to higher education teaching and administration. He has been a school board member in both public and private schools.

Dr. DeRoche is Director of the International Center for Character Education at the University of San Diego and a professor in the School of Education at the University of San Diego. He teaches courses on character education in the graduate program and is Program Director of the Master's Program in Leadership Studies. He served as a member of the National Commission on Character Education for the Association of Teacher Educators. He is a member of the Advisory Board for the National Clearinghouse for the Teaching of Character in Educator Preparation Programs.

Dr. DeRoche is recognized nationally for his work in character education and using daily newspapers for teaching values and ethics. He is a national consultant and speaker on educating the "hearts and minds" of children and youth. He has made many presentations at character education conferences, workshops, and seminars.

His publications on character education and evaluation include many articles and the following books:

How School Administrators Solve Problems. (1985). Prentice-Hall

An Administrator's Guide for Evaluation Programs and Personnel. (1989, 2nd ed.). Allyn & Bacon

Character Matters: Using Newspapers to Teach Character. (1999). Use the News Foundation

Education Hearts and Minds: A Comprehensive Character Education Framework. (2001, 2nd ed.) Corwin Press (co-authored with Dr. Mary Williams)

Character Education: A Guide for School Administrators. (2001). Scarecrow Press (co-authored with Dr. Mary Williams)

Character Education: A Primer for Teachers (2001) Argus Communications (co-authored with Dr. Mary Williams)

About This Book

The scene: A workshop for teachers and administrators on developing and implementing a framework for character education at the school site.

The question: "If we implement a character education program, how will we know if our efforts will pay off?" This is the first of my "frequently asked questions." The other four are:

"How do we find the time to do character education?"
"What program do you recommend?"
"Whose values are we to teach?"
"How do we do it?"

As you know, no two schools are the same, even in the same school district. All schools have their own "personality." So to account for the variation in schools, and thus their character education efforts, this book offers guidelines and principles about character education evaluation at the school site.

The book is designed to meet the needs of readers, like you, who want to evaluate character education efforts and need some direction. It is for educators who want to be responsible for character education assessment and accountability. It includes ideas, suggestions, and examples of ways to evaluate specific elements of character education efforts. It provides you and other character education leaders, whether an individual or a group, with step-by-step ways to focus on self-evaluation using inventories, questionnaires, surveys, focus groups, scales, checklists and other evaluation strategies for data collection and decision making. Some of the material in this book may have to be adapted to meet the unique situational factors at your school.

Audience

This book is intended for teachers, administrators, and character education committees at the school site. My purpose is to help school-site personnel evaluate their character education efforts. My focus is on you—the teacher, the principal, parents and students, the support staff, and the school's character education evaluation committee who on a daily basis work diligently to model your school's core values.

This book may also be of interest to central office professionals who are responsible for evaluating district-wide character education initiatives. I hope K-12 teachers, administrators, counselors, and parent-leaders also find it valuable and useful.

Is Too—Is Not!

While this book provides valuable information about evaluating character education at the school site, it is not all-inclusive. It will not make you (or the committee) an evaluation expert. To paraphrase Daniel Stufflebeam: For school personnel at a school site who want to evaluate their own work and efforts, my opinion is that evaluation is best looked at, not necessarily as a way to prove something, but to improve something.[1]

Evaluation of character education, broadly defined, is to assess its worth and merit and to collect and use information for helping realize the goals of the school's character education initiatives. This book will start you on the evaluation journey and take you a few miles down the road. It will help you appreciate the need for, the importance of, and the "power" of character education evaluation. It is designed to encourage evaluation and promote its worth. It offers examples and ideas that will help you and your colleagues determine what works, what doesn't, and what has to be changed in your efforts to enhance the character of students at your school.

This book may be the beginning for establishing standards for a school's character education efforts. Some of the instruments are standards-driven, but they use synonyms for words such as principles and guidelines. It is clear in this age of school accountability that someone or some group will ask you and your colleagues to justify (account for) the time and energy spent trying to develop the character of students at the school. The data generated by the instruments in this book might help in your accountability efforts. They will certainly inform the processes and programmatic initiatives that are used in your school.

Design

Conversations with professionals, some experts, and many teachers and administrators about character education at the school site have led me to believe that the best way to help them is to try to answer five essential evaluation questions asked of me time and time again:

What should we evaluate?
When should we evaluate?
Who should do the evaluation?
How should we evaluate?
What do we do with the results?

I usually add a sixth question: Why do it? This book is designed to answer these questions.

In Part I, you will read my views and assumptions about evaluating character education under Evaluation Suggestions. Practical, easy-to-use Evaluation Strategies are found in Part II. Each one is an SES—a sample evaluation strategy.

The book concludes with resources (more instruments and readings) for your school's character education library.

Contents

PART I

Evaluation Suggestions

ES 1
Organize Now

Each school should have a character education evaluation committee (CEEC). Membership on the committee depends on the size of the school, but it should represent as many of the stake holders as possible—teachers, administrators, classified personnel, parents, students, and community members. For example, some large schools have a character education council and two subcommittees—one for evaluation and another for partnerships. Other schools have two committees—one responsible for all of the school's character education efforts and another for evaluation work. Smaller schools have one committee that does it all. The point is that evaluation work requires organization, leadership, and resources.

ES 2
"You Gotta Know the Territory"

So said the salesman in the musical *The Music Man*. "Knowing the territory" means that CEEC members are continually educating themselves about character education literature and research. For evaluation, I recommend beginning with the resources listed in the endnotes and "Evaluation Library" section of this book.

Committee members look through the table of contents for the evaluation strategies that will best meet their needs. Before they make a selection, they examine recommended resources, discuss options, and decide what to do. In some cases, they may use the evaluation strategies as presented. In other cases, they may change or modify them. They may even reject the sample instruments, and instead use instruments and techniques suggested by the resources they have consulted. Or, they may use the evaluation strategies and the resources together, designing their own plan, employing their own evaluation methods, and creating their own instruments.

That's how this book should be used—to inform, to launch the exploration, to generate new ideas, to create discussions, and then to evaluate!

ES 3
The School Site

Here is what I said in the early eighties: "Experience and common sense suggest that if education is to do the things we say it should do, it must be accomplished at the building level.... Educational change will be most effective when it resides with the principal, teachers, students, and parents in the individual school" (p. 4).[2]

Twenty years later, I repeat that character education initiatives are school specific. Just as no two homes our students come from are the same, the schools that they come to are not the same. Each school, even in the same district, has its own unique cultural, economic, and social characteristics. Even where a school district has a district-wide character education program, each school puts its individual spin on that program. This being the case, character education evaluation is also school-specific and should be carried out by people, like you, at each school.

ES 4
Purpose of Evaluation

A school's character education efforts must be related to goals, outcomes, and expectations. The value in eVALUation is the collection of data to determine the extent to which each of these three components has been attained.

The school's character education efforts are evaluated so that stake holders can examine, verify, modify, and/or correct the content, the processes, and the outcomes of their work. Stake holders evaluate to find out the extent to which the school's character education efforts affect relationships, learning, teaching, student behavior, and the school's culture. You and the CEEC need to understand that data informs decisions. Data meets the accountability needs of the district and your school. Data drives improvement efforts.

The purpose of evaluating your school's character education efforts is to gather information for determining what works and what doesn't, to collect information for problem solving and for making informed decisions.

ES 5

Benefits of Evaluation

What are the benefits of school-site evaluation to you and your colleagues at school? What benefits result from developing your own evaluation plans? I suggest that there are four benefits:

1. **Enhanced relationships:** The process of evaluation contributes to the development of positive, collaborative relationships.

2. **Ownership:** The process strengthens the ownership of the character education mission and goals, and it strengthens interest to find out what is working and what needs to be changed.

3. **Community of learners:** The process brings stake holders together to learn, practice, apply, and value evaluation techniques and strategies.

4. **Empowerment:** The process empowers school personnel, including students, to value self-evaluation and self-reflection.

ES 6

Data-Savvy Committee

The school's character education committee can become "data savvy" by following these four steps which are a modification of suggestions from an article on data-driven schools.[3]

• **Identify questions that focus on factors to be evaluated.** For example, with regard to questions about student behavior, the committee might ask: How do students act in classrooms? In the hallways? On buses? On the playground? In assemblies? At sporting events?

• **Collect data—information that will help answer these questions.** Take into account any variables such as gender, race, age, grade level, home factors, instructional and school factors, socioeconomic factors, and so on. This is called disaggregating the data, that is, looking at the data by specific categories.

• **Study the data.** Does it tell you about current school or classroom practices that may lead to misbehaviors or good behaviors? Does it target students that may need special help and support? Does it tell the committee how the school's core values influence the school's climate or student behaviors?

• **Ask more questions.** What is the relationship between behavior and achievement? Between character development efforts and achievement? Does the data suggest trends? Are there current initiatives that might improve student behavior? Are there implications for more services, for differing instructional practices, for changes in school policies and practices? Do the findings suggest the need for staff development? For intervention programs?

ES 7
Timetable

Tread carefully, proceed cautiously, plan appropriately. You (the committee) cannot and should not evaluate everything in one year. My suggestion is that no more than two or three components of a school's character education efforts should be assessed in any single school year. Time is at a premium because the people doing the evaluation have primary responsibilities teaching or administering. In many cases, evaluation committee work is seen as, and actually is, an add-on, albeit a very important one. I have found that while teachers and others take on the responsibilities of serving on the school's character education committees with enthusiasm, dedication, and resolve, they frequently get burned out and frustrated because they tried to take on too much in a short period of time.

ES 8
Researchers vs. Practitioners

Character education researchers and teachers/administrators have different reasons and interests for evaluating character education efforts in schools. Researchers are concerned about methodology, generalizability, randomization, and transfer effects. Teachers and administrators do not have the luxury of time, nor the resources to do what researchers require.

School personnel only have time to be concerned about the academic and character development of the students in their school for as long as the students are in that school. You and your colleagues are concerned about student behavior, school culture, safety, instruction, and performance. I like to apply what I call the "family principle" to do-it-yourself evaluation work. That is, the best that a school or home can do for each child is to provide a supportive, caring, civil, challenging, virtue-based environment. The hope is that when the child leaves school and home, he/she will practice the virtues you tried to teach them.

While the evaluation recommendations in this book will not meet all of the requirements of researchers, they will meet the purposes of "responsive evaluation"[4], which means that stake holders are engaged in questions about program efforts employing a variety of quantitative and qualitative methods that seek answers to their questions. It means that they respond by sharing the information with all of the school's stake holders. "We who take the 'responsive evaluation' approach complete our studies without strong proof that the program was a success or failure and even without hard data for making good comparisons—but we often end up with people understanding their program better" (p. 54).

Gordon Vessels said it best: "You (teachers, principals, committees) are therefore advised to keep your evaluation in-house, simple, manageable and leave...(research) designs...to researchers whose purposes go beyond the goals and objectives of your school" (p. 168).[5]

ES 9:
Outside Evaluators

Outside evaluators cannot and should not assume the committee's evaluation responsibilities. They can, however, help verify what the committee says are the school's character education goals, expectations, outcomes and progress.

Most schools use outside evaluators for accrediting purposes, so this process is not new to you. Several intervention programs use "expert panels" to judge the quality of a program. The U.S. Department of Education and the Character Education Partnership use outside evaluators to determine award-winning character education schools. In each case, the first step is the "paper screening," the self-study, the self-report. Pass the paper screening, and the next step is a visit by a panel of experts. Outside opinions about the quality and effectiveness of your school's character education initiatives are useful and informative.

Meg Korpi[6] provides excellent suggestions and guidelines for hiring an outside evaluator, with web sites addressing principles, standards, and practices of evaluation.

ES 10
Action Research Team Focus

It is exciting and rewarding to see teachers, administrators, and support staff (and in some cases, classified personnel and students) come together to do their own research. That's what action research is all about—investigating, examining, and studying school and classroom problems, events, behaviors, and outcomes by those directly involved in the daily life of the school. When the school's character education committee encourages and supports action research, it expands the talent pool for evaluation.

How best to do this? I suggest that the character education committee begins the process by preparing the stake holders for action research. Reflective readings and discussion sessions should be centered on such books as:

- James McLean's *Improving Education Through Action Research* (Corwin Press, 1995).
- Joanne Ahar, Mary Holly and Wendy Kasten's *Action Research for Teachers: Traveling the Yellow Brick Road* (Prentice-Hall, 2001).
- *Education Week* (6-12-02) has an informative four-page article with the headline "Holding Up A Mirror." The subhead tells the story: "Teacher-Researchers Use Their Own Classrooms to Investigate Questions."

When all are ready, the CEEC should identify the resources and rewards that will be made available to individuals and teams who wish to engage in action research. Projects should be submitted and approved by the committee. Team projects get preference. Why? Mike Schmoker[7] makes the case that schools perform better when teachers work in teams, and that teachers do more by working in teams than by working individually in isolation from one another.

Team research projects investigating aspects of the school's character education effort lead to team inquiry, reflection, and action. Here are three examples:

1. Several teachers instituted class meetings as part of their character education plans. They now want to find out if these meetings have had any effect on the climate in their classrooms and on the behavior of their students.

2. A team of teachers and administrators (and two students) is interested in determining whether students are using the "language of virtues" (school's core virtues) in their interactions with adults and classmates.

3. Another team of teachers wants to apply a set of program/curriculum standards to commercial character education programs that they may recommend for purchase.

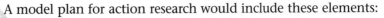

A model plan for action research would include these elements:

- Research questions, hypotheses, or descriptions of the problem(s) to be investigated
- Methods to be used to find answers to the questions/hypotheses
- The audience, documents, artifacts, or other sources that will be used for data collection
- Verification that what is found is accurate and reliable (triangulation)
- Data analysis—what do the findings suggest for action (conclusions and recommendations)

Most individual or team reports should go to the committee for review before being disseminated to others.

Action research, using a team approach, is a powerful way to evaluate many of the elements in character education. Joseph Senese[8] tells of two teachers from Highland Park High School (Illinois), one a Spanish teacher, the other a social studies teacher, joining together with 25 students for a "community of learners." He describes the seven-year-old Action Research Laboratory. Information about the action research program can be found on the high school's web site at www.d113.lake.k12.il.us/hphs/action/table_of_contents.htm.

Another interesting story comes from an article in *Science and Children*[9]. Seventh grade teacher Anne Keith tells the story, which I'm summarizing, of seven teachers from rural Montana schools who came together under the direction of an education professor to work on ways to improve science achievement of students in their schools. Each teacher received a modest stipend ($500) to participate in this professional development opportunity. In the summer, they began by reading Richard Sagor's booklet *How to Conduct Collaborative Action Research*[10], which offers a step-by-step approach to action research. Weekly sessions of two or more hours were held in teachers' homes, where they discussed a five-step action-research process—problem formulation, data collection, data analysis, results reporting, and action planning.

As the author noted, the most important and most difficult part of the process that the teachers engaged in was formulating the right questions. Group meetings and teacher-pair meetings resulted in refining, reflecting, and revising the questions that the teachers would research. During data collection the teachers followed the "triangulation" process, collecting "three pieces of data needed to answer the questions" from the pool of data collected (p. 34). In the action phase of the process, one group of teachers created ways to engage students in science projects and presentations while also involving them in helping the teachers create an assessment rubric.

In closing the article, the author points to the enthusiasm that these rural teachers exhibited during this professional development opportunity. She describes how the process "empowered teachers to continue making changes within their classrooms." Teachers reported that in building the "community of scholars," they became better at their work and that the interactions with each other was the best part of the project (p.35).

My suggestion is to capitalize on the value of action research, as these teachers did, and reflect on the following five questions gleaned from the article summary:

What does the story tell you?
What does it suggest for professional development?
What does it say about action research?
What does it say about teachers collaborating with one another?
What are the implications for evaluating character education?

ES 11
Two Kinds of Evaluation

You have heard of summative and formative evaluation, but it's worth repeating here. Formative evaluation is a process whereby you and the committee gather data and use the information while carrying out character education plans and projects. It is ongoing, providing continuous feedback that informs your plans and decisions. It answers the question "How is it working?"

Summative evaluation usually occurs at the end of a program, activity, or plan. It answers the question "How did it work?" It does not offer the opportunity for changing or fine-tuning a plan, activity, or project while it is being implemented.

Information from both formative and summative evaluation of the school's character education efforts leads to one of three decisions—continue, change, cancel! Some of the evaluation strategies in this book may be used with either type of evaluation. Decide whether you want information as you go along or whether you want it at the end. You probably will want both, which means you have to decide which instruments fit your evaluation purposes and timeline.

ES 12
Question Asking

The premise of this book is that good questions elicit useful data that fosters informed decisions. I am of the opinion that question-asking is the *sine qua non* for evaluating the multiple components of a school's character education initiatives. Questions underscore the use of such evaluation "tools" as testimonials, observations, journals, focus groups, surveys, interviews, and activity logs. Questions set the stage for investigating a range of quantitative data such as performance reports, discipline referrals, absentee rates, and behavior reports.

Here is how one author states it[11]:

Question-asking is the "camera" you will use for evaluating the character education efforts.... As you analyze them, the story will delight you, concern you, and challenge you. The point is that you are doing an evaluation for two purposes: to find what is working and what is not; to decide what to retain and what to change (p. 281).

In *Tracking Your School's Success: A Guide to Sensible Evaluation*[12], authors Joan Herman and Lynn Winters say, "[T]racking [I call this mapping] is designed to answer two simple questions: How are we doing? How can we improve? If we add to these two questions 'How can we share our successes?' we have captured the purpose of school-based evaluation" (p. 7-8).

The Character Education Partnership, a nonpartisan coalition of organizations and individuals concerned about the character development of America's children and youth, publishes a booklet on evaluation that is based on answers to a list of evaluation questions such as:

Do you really know what program evaluation is?

Who will be the audience for your evaluation results?

What do you want to assess?

What types of data will you collect?

What types of measurement instruments can you use?[13]

Solid, penetrating, thoughtful questions underscore self-evaluation. The answers revealed support self-reflection. Both contribute to self-improvement.

ES 13
Data Collection Tool Box

This book offers a variety of "homemade" evaluation instruments designed to provide the committee with a "snapshot" of the school's character education efforts. Some of the instruments have been used in schools; others have not. There are standardized instruments that can be used for some of the components of a school's character education efforts (school climate, for example) that are referenced in this book.

There are many ways for the CEEC to collect information about the school's character education efforts. Think of a box filled with "tools" that you (the committee) can use to collect data. Many of these tools will be used in the evaluation strategies suggested in Part II. Here are some evaluative techniques that are in the "tool box" for use by the school's character education committee.

testimonials	observations	anecdotes and stories
interviews	surveys	focus groups
journals and logs	school reports	case studies
tests	performance data	mapping activities
portfolios	videos	photographs
shadowing	rating scales	checklists and inventories
questionnaires	benchmarking	school records
essays		

I suggest that the CEEC members also read the data collection recommendations in CEP's Evaluation Tool Kit (see endnote 6, pp. 27-39).

ES 14
Triangulation

When collecting data about a particular aspect of the school's character education efforts, think "triangulation." This means using multiple measures rather than single or dual sources of data. This helps when you do not have the opportunity for randomization. It also adds to the validity and reliability of the information you are collecting.

Two examples may be helpful in clarifying this idea.

1. The evaluation committee might find three sources of data for assessing school climate (teachers, supervisors, students) and then compare each of the three to determine the extent to which there is congruence.

2. A teacher wants to evaluate her use of cooperative learning (a key character education instructional component). She might (a) ask a colleague to observe her class, (b) videotape sessions and do a self-evaluation, and (c) interview the class or individual students.

In both cases, there are three sources of information. The committee and the teacher can examine the data to identify similarities and discrepancies.

That's triangulation, and that's what any evaluation committee should try to do most of the time before making public any definitive statements about the results of the school's character education initiatives. It is always wise to follow the carpenter's motto: "Measure twice, cut once!" In this case, measure three times!

ES 15
Data Analysis

It is what you do with what you collect that counts. That means that data keeps no better than fresh fish—you have to use it! The committee must analyze the data for information that clearly answers the questions they posed before data collection. The committee must decide whether to disaggregate the data (examine the findings for different subgroups—grade level, gender, etc.) in order to fine-tune the information collected. The committee must also decide whether the data:

- can be used as a baseline to map trends;
- can be used for comparison purposes (comparing findings with similar schools in the district);
- can be used to determine the degree to which a standard may or may not have been met; or
- simply informs them, as collected, about a component or element in the school's character education efforts.

The point is that the character education committee must use evaluation data to make informed decisions and meaningful school or programmatic changes.

ES 16
Reporting

I believe that evaluation efforts are meaningless if the results are not shared with the stake holders at the school and in the community. Effectively communicating the findings and what they mean to the school's character education stake holders is essential to its continuance and improvement. Reporting results can be educative. Results can encourage discussion and openness. Results can elicit support and service.

The committee can report findings in many different ways, including reports, newsletters, meetings, videos, and letters. Communication is a two-way process, however, so recipients of the results must have an opportunity to respond. The CEP's Tool Kit offers these recommendations for reporting findings (see endnote 6, pp. 44-46):

- State program goals
- Explain the evaluation design
- Summarize key findings
- Open the discussion to the audience
- State evaluation goals
- Report results
- Propose next steps

ES 17
Action Plans

If the committee's purpose for evaluating the school's character education efforts is to determine the impact of the program on student behavior, school climate, in-school relationships, and the extent to which goals and expectations have been reached, then it follows that the findings should lead to action. That

Evaluating Character Development

is, what does the information suggest for change, for improvement, for next steps? What processes and procedures need attention? What did the information tell you that was unexpected? These questions calls for "doing something" with the results. It calls for administrative leadership and support.

Evaluation West Virginia Style

In January 2001, the Office of Student Services and Assessment of the West Virginia Department of Education published a Request for Quotation (RFQ) for the evaluation of character education in West Virginia schools and schools systems. Two types of evaluation were required in the RFQ. The first, process evaluation, asked: Is the character education initiative being implemented as intended? The second was an outcome requirement: What are the effects of the character education initiatives?

For review purposes, the West Virginia character education model is one that uses an integrative, comprehensive approach to "promote the understanding and inspire the development of the general character traits of respect, responsibility, caring, citizenship, justice and fairness, and trustworthiness." The model also utilizes the existing school curricula along with intervention programs, projects, and activities such as peer mediation, conflict resolution, and life skills training.

The RFQ called for a two-phase evaluation design. In Phase I, the evaluators had to provide a profile describing two things:

- how school systems have integrated character education into the curriculum
- how the program impacts data routinely collected by schools and schools systems including but not limited to achievement, attendance, school satisfaction survey, incidents of harassment and violence, safe school violations (weapons reports), and suspensions and expulsions

The Phase I evaluation components had to include an evaluation design with sample surveys, interviewer questionnaires, etc.; descriptions indicating how evidence of character traits are identified in schools and school systems using at least three methods of measurement (e.g., observation, survey, small groups, etc.); descriptions of school-site visits, surveys, observations, and interviews with students, staff, administrators, parents, and community members; evidence that the evaluator has addressed the eleven principles of character education and the character traits listed above; and evidence that the evaluator has addressed the following components:

- Honesty
- Citizenship
- Fairness
- Responsibility
- Academic achievement
- Improving daily attendance
- Alternatives to violence
- Participating in class
- Resisting social peer pressures to smoke, drink, and use drugs

- Caring
- Justice
- Respect
- Voting
- Completing homework assignments
- Avoiding and resolving conflicts
- Contributing to an orderly positive school environment
- Developing greater self-esteem and self-confidence

- Effectively coping with social anxiety
- Increasing the knowledge of the consequences of one's actions
- The value of decent, honest work
- Increasing knowledge of the immediate consequence of substance abuse
- The corrupting influence and chance nature of gambling

The Phase I evaluation report also had to include the following components:

- Summary of the comparison of pre- and post-test character education implementation data
- Brief description of the general background and evolution of character education, identifying each of the school system's character education goals
- Description of links with other school activities and operations
- School system profiles on how character education was implemented into the curriculum, with attention to each of the character traits
- Descriptions of new and existing projects, programs, and activities incorporated into the districts comprehensive character education efforts
- Summary and analysis of the character education documents, staff development and training for each school system

Phase II called for a report on the twenty-five pilot sites (over the next five years) which would include, but not be limited to, a model for comparing pre- and post-test implementation data using a questionnaire/survey that identifies the percentage of students who have demonstrated behaviors that include, but are not limited to, the following:

- Used physical force against another person
- Teased someone because of race and ethnicity
- Taken illegal drugs
- Broken into another's property
- Taken something without paying for it
- Defaced or vandalized property
- Cheated on exams
- Received a detention or suspension
- Missed class without a legitimate excuse
- Let someone copy his or her work
- Lied to a teacher
- Failed to get school work completed on time

The proposal also had to include a profile of the background and evolution of character education at the school sites.

If you have read this proposal carefully, you will note several things that are important to the purpose of this book and for the evaluation of character education at your school.

1. The design calls for a profile and descriptions.
2. It asks for existing "hard data."
3. It proposes a pre- and post-research design method.
4. It is specific about the items and virtues to be assessed.
5. It seeks information about staff development and training.

6. It seeks information about character education that may be imbedded in school documents and policies.

7. While it addresses character education at the school district level, it offers many helpful suggestions that school-site personnel can use for their own evaluation plans.

Endnotes

1. Stufflebeam, D. "The CIPP Model for Evaluation." in D. Stufflebeam, G. Madaus, and T. Kellaghan. *Evaluation Models: Viewpoints on Educational and Human Services Evaluation*. Boston: (Kluwer Academic Publishers, 2000).

2. DeRoche, E. *An Administrator's Guide to Evaluating School Programs and Personnel*. (Boston: Allyn & Bacon, 1981).

3. Noyce, P. Perda, D. and Traver, R. "Creating Data-Driven Schools," *Educational Leadership*, 57 (February 2000): 55-58.

4. Stake, R. and Hoke, G. "Evaluating an Arts Program: Movement and Dance in a Downtown District," *National Elementary School Principal*, 55 (January/February 1976): 52-59.

5. Vessels, G. *Character and Community Development: A School Planning and Teacher Training Handbook*. (Wesport, Conn.: Praeger, 1998).

6. Korpi, M. "Hiring an Outside Evaluator for a Character Education Program." In J.Posey, and M. Davidson. *Character Education Evaluation Toolkit*. Washington, D.C.: The Character Education Partnership.

7. Schmoker, M. *Results: The Key to Continuous Improvement*. (Alexandria, Va.: Association for Supervision and Curriculum Development, 1996).

8. Senese, J. "Energize With Action Research." *Journal of Staff Development*. 23, 3: 39-41.

9. Keith, A. "Action Research Brings Results," *Science and Children*, 39 (November/December 2001): 32-35.

10. Sagor, R. *How to Conduct Action Research*. (Alexandria, Va.: Association for Supervision and Curriculum Development, 1992).

11. Jeroski, S. "Finding Out What We Need to Know." In A.Costa, J. Bellanca, and R.Fogarty (eds.), *If Minds Matter: A Foreword to the Future, VII*, (Palatine, Ill.: IRI/Skylight Publishing, 1992).

12. Herman, J. and Winters, L. *Tracking Your School's Success: A Guide to Sensible Evaluation*. (Thousand Oaks, Calif.: Corwin Press, 1992).

13. Berkowitz, M. *A Primer for Evaluating a Character Education Initiative*. (Washington, D.C.: The Character Education Partnership, n.d.).

PART II

Sample Evaluation Strategies

An examination of recent research and best practices suggests that most schools' character education programs are guided by a framework that includes many of the components suggested in the three examples below.

Example 1

Ryan and Bohlin, in *Building Character in Schools* (San Francisco: Jossey-Bass, 1999) offer a framework for character education that includes these components:

- mission
- partnerships
- staff development
- integrating activities
- teamwork implementation
- core virtues
- meetings and assessment
- student involvement
- evaluation

Example 2

In my article "Creating a Framework for Character Education," in *Principal*, the journal for the National Association of Elementary School Principals (January 2000: 32-34), I noted 10 components of a character education framework:

- values
- expectations
- resources
- partnerships
- assessment standards
- vision
- leadership
- training
- programs standards
- implementation standards

Example 3

The framework proposed, by DeRoche and Williams, in *Educating Hearts and Minds: A Comprehensive Character Education Framework* (Thousand Oaks, Calif.: Corwin Press, 2001) identifies nine keys to successful character education efforts:

- leadership
- school climate
- standards
- partnerships
- expectations/consensus.
- assessment
- implementation criteria
- training
- resources

Let's address the question of HOW [we evaluate a program]. The following sample evaluation strategies center on elements in a framework that unlocks the potential for creating, implementing, maintaining, and evaluating character education content, processes, and products at the school site.

Evaluation strategies should center on the components within your school's character education framework, regardless of which one is used at your school (and you do have one, whether you realize it or not!). In fact, a good initial evaluation strategy is to take any one of the three frameworks in the examples above and note how many components are part of your school's character education initiatives.

How should the evaluation strategies be implemented?

Step 1

Start with the last component—EVALUATION—because it provides questions, guidelines, and principles that will be important to you and the committee as the evaluation plans begin.

Step 2

Go sequentially, beginning with the ORGANIZATION/ADMINISTRATION component. Use any of the sample instruments (as is or modified) in each component that best suits your immediate needs. Then lay out an evaluation plan and see if the other instruments will help you get the information you need to accomplish your purposes. *Note that many of the instruments you and the character education evaluation committee (CEEC) use may require the permission of the respondents. If the respondents are students, parent permission may be necessary.*

Step 3

Finally, and most importantly, be flexible. How you and/or the school's CEEC proceed depends on needs, interests, and the length of time the character education initiatives have been in place. Evaluation needs and plans will be different for a new character education program than for one that has been operating in a school for three or more years.

Section 1 | Organization and Administration

It should be clear by now that there must be a committee responsible for implementing, maintaining, and evaluating character development efforts at the school site. The size of the school (i.e., the number of personnel) will determine the number of committees to be created to do the school's character education work. In some large schools, there may be three committees—a character education council, a character education partnership committee, and a character education evaluation committee—the latter two reporting to the council. In moderate-size schools, there may be only two committees. In smaller schools, one committee will be responsible for leading and managing all of the school's character education initiatives.

The framework below is recommended for your school's character education evaluation committee (CEEC). It may serve as useful template. The questions in this evaluation strategy should be reviewed throughout the year to guide discussion and action plans.

SES 1-1
Framework

Mission
Does or will the school's character education efforts include a mission statement? If not, why not?

Values
Has the school community selected a set of core values/virtues that will permeate character education programs and activities and the school culture?

Leadership
Is the leadership for the program such that it empowers stake holders? Does teamwork permeate the organization? Are students and parents included?

Partnerships
Are partnerships with parents/guardians and the community a key component of the school's character education efforts?

Implementation
Has the committee developed plans for implementing, maintaining, and evaluating its character education efforts?

Training
Have staff development plans been made for training all school personnel for their work in the program?

Resources
Have time and money been allotted so that stake holders can engage in meetings, training, visitations, review of curriculum materials, and other enriching activities to prepare them for their work in the character development of students at the school?

Programs
Have stake holders selected or created appropriate programs and activities that integrate the core values into the curriculum and extracurricular activities of the school?

Evaluation
Has the leadership developed plans for assessing the goals, expectations, and outcomes of the school's character education efforts?

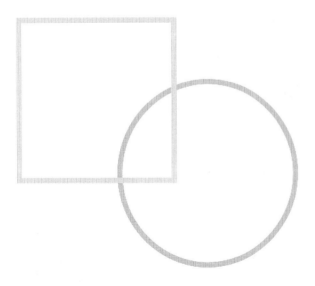

Evaluating Character Development

SES 1-2
Organizing Questions

A school's character education committee needs guidance and direction before launching into evaluation plans and strategies. One way to do this is to "map" the work that the committee needs to do in the form of questions. The committee's answers to these questions will determine their readiness for the tasks ahead.

Readiness Questions

1. Has consensus been reached among stake holders regarding readiness to engage in evaluation?
2. What background information will be needed before the evaluation is implemented?
3. What partnerships should be established before the evaluation begins (parents, colleges, school district offices, community agencies)?
4. What resources will be needed to implement evaluation plans?

Implementation Questions

1. What should be evaluated?
2. Why should it be evaluated?
3. What is the evaluation timeline?
4. What instruments or assessment techniques will be used?
5. Who will be involved in the evaluation? Have they been informed?
6. How will evaluation information be collected?
7. Who will be responsible for collating the data?
8. Who will be responsible for interpreting the data?
9. Will outside assistance be needed for data collection and interpretation?

Reporting/Action Questions

1. How will the data be reported to the stake holders?
2. How will the stake holders provide feedback?
3. Who will be responsible for developing any action plans resulting from the evaluation?
4. What will be the committee's next steps?

SES 1-3
Leadership Standards Scale

Effective school leadership capitalizes on collaboration and teamwork. Look at the research. On the academic side, evidence suggests that when teachers and others come together to use their "intellectual capital" to bring new ideas and recommendations to solve problems, there are gains in student achievement; higher quality solutions to problems; greater ability to examine, expand, and test new ideas, methods, and materials. There is also stronger support for each others' strengths and an accommodation of weaknesses.

John Little, "The Persistence of Privacy: Autonomy and Initiative in Teachers' Professional Relations," *Teachers College Record*

The school's administrators and the character education committee should use the team approach to engage others in evaluating the school's character education efforts. Teams will bring to the evaluative process stake holders with a variety of talents, skills, and experiences that enhance the resources necessary to get tasks accomplished. If you need a motto, it should be: Collaborate to Evaluate!

Implementing the motto requires leadership. The leadership for character education at the school site, for the most part, must come from the school principal. The nature of this position, its status and responsibilities, requires that the school principal play a key role in the character development of students and in the character initiatives at the school. No school's character education efforts will meet its goals and expectations without leadership. In this evaluation strategy, the focus is on the leadership provided by the school's administrators and by the school's character education committee.

The school's character education leaders must be the visionaries, directing initiatives toward intended goals and outcomes, designing programs and activities, educating stake holders, encouraging participation, involving parents and students, tapping community resources, and, of course, taking the time to develop effective and informative evaluation methods. There are two leadership principles for principals:

1. **Lead by example and manage by values.**
2. **Leadership earned is leadership shared.**

For this evaluation strategy, the word administration will be used because in many schools the leadership for the character education program has been delegated to other administrators other than the principal (committee, assistant principal, lead teacher).

The following scale is intended as a self-evaluation instrument to be used by stake holders to assess the leadership in charge of the school's character education efforts.

Respondent:
☐ Administrator ☐ Committee member ☐ Teacher
☐ Counselor ☐ Other (specify) _____

Directions: For each standard listed below, rate both the school administrator's and the character education committee's leadership for supporting and implementing the standard. Check all items that apply to each standard.

Standard 1: *There is a vision and mission for this school's character education initiatives.*

Administration's leadership for this standard is

- ☐ powerful
- ☐ visible
- ☐ adequate
- ☐ hidden
- ☐ weak
- ☐ needs attention

Committee leadership for this standard is

- ☐ powerful
- ☐ visible
- ☐ adequate
- ☐ hidden
- ☐ weak
- ☐ needs attention

Standard 2: *There is an effective organizational plan for this school's character education efforts.*

Administration's leadership for this standard is

- ☐ powerful
- ☐ visible
- ☐ adequate
- ☐ hidden
- ☐ weak
- ☐ needs attention

Committee leadership for this standard is

- ☐ powerful
- ☐ visible
- ☐ adequate
- ☐ hidden
- ☐ weak
- ☐ needs attention

Standard 3: *The goals and expectations are kept at the forefront of the program.*

Administration's leadership for this standard is

- ☐ powerful
- ☐ visible
- ☐ adequate
- ☐ hidden
- ☐ weak
- ☐ needs attention

Committee leadership for this standard is

- ☐ powerful
- ☐ visible
- ☐ adequate
- ☐ hidden
- ☐ weak
- ☐ needs attention

Standard 4: *The core values are modeled and practiced.*

Administration's leadership for this standard is

- ☐ powerful
- ☐ visible
- ☐ adequate
- ☐ hidden
- ☐ weak
- ☐ needs attention

Committee leadership for this standard is

- ☐ powerful
- ☐ visible
- ☐ adequate
- ☐ hidden
- ☐ weak
- ☐ needs attention

Standard 5: *Resources are provided for all aspects of this school's character education efforts.*

Administration's leadership for this standard is

- ☐ powerful
- ☐ visible
- ☐ adequate
- ☐ hidden
- ☐ weak
- ☐ needs attention

Committee leadership for this standard is

- ☐ powerful
- ☐ visible
- ☐ adequate
- ☐ hidden
- ☐ weak
- ☐ needs attention

Standard 6:   *Staff development is supported as an essential component of the program.*

Administration's leadership for this standard is
☐ powerful   ☐ adequate   ☐ weak
☐ visible   ☐ hidden   ☐ needs attention

Committee leadership for this standard is
☐ powerful   ☐ adequate   ☐ weak
☐ visible   ☐ hidden   ☐ needs attention

Standard 7:   *There is clear and consistent communication about the school's character education efforts to all stake holders.*

Administration's leadership for this standard is
☐ powerful   ☐ adequate   ☐ weak
☐ visible   ☐ hidden   ☐ needs attention

Committee leadership for this standard is
☐ powerful   ☐ adequate   ☐ weak
☐ visible   ☐ hidden   ☐ needs attention

Standard 8:   *Rewards and incentives are provided to those who, through their actions, show a commitment to the school's core values and the program mission.*

Administration's leadership for this standard is
☐ powerful   ☐ adequate   ☐ weak
☐ visible   ☐ hidden   ☐ needs attention

Committee leadership for this standard is
☐ powerful   ☐ adequate   ☐ weak
☐ visible   ☐ hidden   ☐ needs attention

Standard 9:   *School policies and practices are driven by the core values and the mission of the school's character education efforts.*

Administration's leadership for this standard is
☐ powerful   ☐ adequate   ☐ weak
☐ visible   ☐ hidden   ☐ needs attention

Committee leadership for this standard is
☐ powerful   ☐ adequate   ☐ weak
☐ visible   ☐ hidden   ☐ needs attention

Standard 10:   *Evaluation of the program and its personnel is seen as an essential component of the school's character education initiative.*

Administration's leadership for this standard is
☐ powerful   ☐ adequate   ☐ weak
☐ visible   ☐ hidden   ☐ needs attention

Committee leadership for this standard is
☐ powerful   ☐ adequate   ☐ weak
☐ visible   ☐ hidden   ☐ needs attention

SES 1-4
Personnel Support Questionnaire

The purpose of this scale is to find out how school personnel view each of the following essential factors regarding the school's character education efforts.

Respondent:

☐ Teacher ☐ Counselor ☐ Administrator
☐ Classified personnel ☐ Other (specify) _____

Directions: Check the choice that best reflects your view and then identify any concerns or make comments that you believe will help the character education evaluation committee.

A. Do school personnel know the mission of this school's character education initiatives?

☐ They certainly do ☐ Some do, some don't ☐ Most do not

Comment _____

_____

B. Do school personnel support the goals of the school's character education efforts?

☐ They certainly do ☐ Some do, some don't ☐ Most do not

Comment _____

_____

C. Are school personnel working together to implement this school's character education programs?

☐ They are; there is much collaboration.
☐ Some are working together; some have opted out.
☐ There is little coordinated effort; most seem to be doing their own thing.

Comment _____

_____

D. Is there a focus by all school personnel on teaching/modeling the monthly core virtues of the program?

☐ We all do our part each month.
☐ Some do it, others don't.
☐ There is no general focus; it's haphazard at best.

Comment _____

_____

E. Are relations among teachers and administrators contributing to the school's character education efforts?

☐ Yes, most definitely.
☐ They are not bad, but could be better.
☐ No, they are strained and divisive.

Comment _____

_____

F. Is the communication about the school's character education program effective, informative, and useful?

☐ Yes, it's very good.

☐ It's fair, though it could be better.

☐ What communication? It's terrible!

Comment _____

_____

G. Is the staff getting the support it needs to implement or maintain a viable, effective character education program?

☐ We have wonderful support, appreciated by all.

☐ We have some support; there could be more.

☐ We have very little support.

Comment _____

_____

H. Are school personnel rewarded for their efforts to foster the character development of students?

☐ Yes, we are adequately rewarded.

☐ There are some rewards, but there are very modest.

☐ No rewards have been forthcoming.

Comment _____

_____

I. In general, how do school personnel feel about the school's character education efforts?

☐ Most feel it is a meaningful part of our efforts to educate the whole student.

☐ Most feel it is an add-on that takes time away from the academics.

☐ Most feel it is a waste of time.

Comment _____

_____

SES 1-5
Benchmarking Rating Scale

Benchmarking is "the process of identifying someone or some organization that is doing something better than you are doing, studying how they are doing it, and adopting these procedures that could be most useful to reach your desired outcome."

J. W. Alstete, "Benchmarking in Higher Education: Adapting Best Practices to Improve Quality," *ASHE-ERIC Higher Education Reports*

Benchmarking is "the study and transfer of specific exemplary practices, measures, and processes from another school or organization to your school...." For example, reducing violence may be part of your school's character education goals. The committee says, "Let's find a school or organization that has had the most success in reducing violence, study, analyze how they achieved success, and adapt those practices in our school."

Sue Tucker, *Benchmarking: A Guide for Educators*

For this evaluation strategy, the concept of benchmarking has been modified. This example will highlight some of the strategies of award-winning high schools. The strategies/activities have been gleaned from the Character Education Partnership's publications of national schools of character and promising practices. This sample strategy focuses on high school practices, but it may be used at other school levels.

The CEEC may wish to review CEP booklets for each of the past five years that describe award-winning schools. The CEEC can then select schools that seem to be a good match, contact these schools, and study their particular character education practices, programs, and products.

For example, suppose the CEEC at your school wants to see what award-winning high schools do in their character education programs. They may use the scale below to compare practices and procedures. Each member of the CEEC completes the inventory and brings his/her ratings to a CEEC meeting. Comparison ratings are the focus of the discussion.

1. The whole community buys into the school's core virtues.
   - ☐ Ours does totally.
   - ☐ Some do, some don't.
   - ☐ Not many do.
   - ☐ We need to work on this.

2. Mission/motto ("To get students ready to be good, productive citizens" or "3Ps-purpose, pride, performance").
   - ☐ We have one.
   - ☐ We could improve what we have.
   - ☐ We don't have one and should.
   - ☐ We don't need one.

3. Virtues are infused in daily life of the school and the curriculum.
   - ☐ We do this very well.
   - ☐ We do this fairly well.
   - ☐ We really need to focus on improving in this area.
   - ☐ We need to find out more about _____.

4. Special courses/projects activities (e.g., counselor-taught life-skills courses, student leadership opportunities, rewards/recognitions from academics to athletics, class meeting, cooperative learning, peer mediation, school newspaper)
   ☐ We have many of these.
   ☐ We need to do more in this area.
   ☐ We need to find out more about _____

5. Staff development (e.g., creation of a character education reading group, discussions about commitment to the program, reflections on what is working and what needs attention, guest speakers, video reviews, visitations)
   ☐ We have limited staff development opportunities.
   ☐ Our staff development efforts have been a waste of time.
   ☐ We are doing this.
   ☐ This is something that really needs our attention.

6. Resources (e.g., character education library, videos, instructional materials, money for conferences/visitations, set of supplemental lessons)
   ☐ We have some of this.
   ☐ We need to enhance our resource efforts.
   ☐ We could do some of this with current resources.
   ☐ We need to find out more about _____

7. School/community projects and service learning (e.g., student-run credit union, STARS (Students Taking Action Reaching Students) counseling elementary and middle grade students, 50-hour community service credit requirement, a full-time community service coordinator, special holiday events, fundraising events)
   ☐ We do some of this. (Identify) _____
   ☐ We could do more of this. (Identify) _____
   ☐ Some of this we can't do. (Identify) _____
   ☐ We should find out more about _____

SES 1-6
Teacher Efficacy

Do teachers feel they have the "power" or capacity to be character educators? Do they believe they can make a difference in the character development of students at the school? To find out, the CEEC could ask teachers to complete the instrument below. The CDEBI was designed by Professors Andrew Milson and James Mehlig and field-tested with 767 elementary schools teachers in a large midwestern suburban school district. The CEEC may use the results to determine the extent to which teachers at the school feel they have the capacity to be effective character educators.

Character Development Efficacy Belief Instrument (CDEBI)*

Directions to the teacher: As you read each of the following statements, please indicate your level of agreement by circling the appropriate letters in the left column.

SA = Strongly Agree   A = Agree   U = Uncertain
D = Disagree   SD = Strongly Disagree

SA   A   U   D   SD   1. I am usually comfortable discussing issues of right and wrong with my students.

SA   A   U   D   SD   2. When a student has been exposed to negative influences at home, I do not believe that I can do much to impact the child's character.

SA   A   U   D   SD   3. I am confident in my ability to be a good role model.

SA   A   U   D   SD   4. Teachers are usually not responsible when a child becomes more courteous.

SA   A   U   D   SD   5. When a student shows greater respect for others, it is usually because teachers have effectively modeled that trait.

SA   A   U   D   SD   6. I am usually at a loss as to how to help a student be more responsible.

SA   A   U   D   SD   7. I know how to use strategies that might lead to positive changes in students' character.

SA   A   U   D   SD   8. I am not sure that I can teach my students to be honest.

SA   A   U   D   SD   9. When students demonstrate diligence, it is often because teachers have encouraged the students to persist with tasks.

SA   A   U   D   SD   10. Teachers who spend time encouraging students to be respectful of others will see little change in students' social interaction.

SA   A   U   D   SD   11. I am able to positively influence the character development of a child who has had little direction from parents.

SA   A   U   D   SD   12. If parents notice that their children are more responsible, it is likely that teachers have fostered this trait at school.

SA   A   U   D   SD   13. Some students will not become more respectful, even if they have had teachers who promote respect.

*Used with permission from Professors Milson and Mehlig. Also see Milson, A. (2001). *Teacher Efficacy and Character Education.* College Park, Md.: ERIC Clearinghouse on Assessment and Evaluation. 32 pp. paper, ED 454 212.

SA A U D SD 14. When I have a student who lies regularly, I usually can convince him to stop lying.

SA A U D SD 15. If students are inconsiderate, it is often because teachers have not sufficiently modeled the trait.

SA A U D SD 16. If responsibility is not encouraged in a child's home, teachers have not sufficiently modeled this trait.

SA A U D SD 17. I often find it difficult to persuade a student that respect for others is important.

SA A U D SD 18. When a student becomes more compassionate, it is usually because teachers have created caring classroom environments.

SA A U D SD 19. I will be able to influence the character of students because I am a good role model.

SA A U D SD 20. Teaching students what it means to be honest is unlikely to result in students who are more honest.

SA A U D SD 21. I sometimes don't know what to do to help students become more compassionate.

SA A U D SD 22. Teachers cannot be blamed for students who are dishonest.

SA A U D SD 23. I am continually finding better ways to develop the character of my students.

SA A U D SD 24. Teachers who encourage responsibility at school can influence students' level of responsibility outside of school.

Scoring

Personal teacher efficacy (PTE) items are 1, 3, 5, 7, 9, 11, 12, 14, 18, 19, 23, 24, and are scored SA=5, A=4, U=3, D=2, SD=1.

General teacher efficacy (GTE) items are 2, 4, 6, 8, 10, 13, 15, 16, 17, 20, 21, 22, and are scored SA=1, A=2, U=3, D=4, SD=5.

Add scores for PTE items—do the same for GTE items. Scores range from 12 to 60 on each scale. Research has shown the average score to be 36.

CEEC may use this instrument in another way. The committee may look at each item and determine how many teachers at the school strongly agreed or agreed with PTE statements and how many disagree or strongly disagree with GTE statements. Such analysis may guide content for an in-service program or two.

SES 1-7
Staff Development Session Evaluation Form

When dealing with character education, special consideration must be given to staff development. The intent is to enhance knowledge and understandings of character education and the character development of children and youth. To be models and mentors of the school's core values, stake holders need to engage in a range of ways to study, learn, and practice.

Staff development encompasses opportunities for stake holders to attend meetings, go to conferences, participate in workshops, enroll in college courses, engage in self-study, visit award-winning character education schools, interact with consultants, and participate in action research projects. At minimum, each school should have a character education library that includes books, videos, and journal articles. (See resources for evaluation at end of the book.)

Staff development means observing, participating, reading, and reporting. It means discussions and debates, teamwork, collaboration, and networking. It means that school personnel, particularly the members of the school's character education committee, should be familiar with the research. It helps inform their evaluation efforts and program plans.

Staff development efforts should do these things: 1) contribute to the skills and abilities of school personnel to integrate the school's core values into the curriculum; 2) make them integral to classroom relationships and instruction; 3) develop school-wide activities that support them; and 4) have them be a natural part of the daily life of the school. Staff development should also inform school personnel on how best to implement, maintain, and evaluate their efforts to develop the character of students at their school. The following form may be useful in evaluating staff development sessions about character education matters.

Dear Participant: This form will be used to evaluate all of our staff development opportunities this year. We ask that you complete the form following each session and return it to a member of the CEEC committee, or drop it off in the box located in the session room.

Topic of Session _____   Date of Session _____

Location of Session _____   Time of Session _____

Directions: Place a check mark at the point between the two words that represents your views about this session.

Active	____	____	____	____	____	Passive
Interesting	____	____	____	____	____	Boring
Useful	____	____	____	____	____	Worthless
Thoughtless	____	____	____	____	____	Thoughtful
Informative	____	____	____	____	____	Uninformative
Unprepared	____	____	____	____	____	Prepared
Bad	____	____	____	____	____	Good
Recommended	____	____	____	____	____	Not Recommended

Please complete each item below:

1. This character education session _____
_____
_____
_____

2. The value of this session is _____
_____
_____
_____

3. To improve this session, I would _____
_____
_____
_____

4. What we really need is _____
_____
_____
_____

<table>
<tr><td>

Section 2

</td><td>

Mission and Values

</td></tr>
</table>

The foundation of an effective organization [is] its mission and values.

Ken Blanchard and Mark O'Connor, *Managing by Values*

...They've been told not to put anything in the mission statement...that isn't "measurable." So they shy away from things like character education.... We just need to stretch our vocabulary from "measurable" to "observable."

Edie Holcomb, *Getting Excited About Data*

Dreams are missions. Missions are ideals that guide behavior, actions, and practices. An organization's mission and values tells what it's all about. Major businesses "live or die" by their mission statements and values (ethical practices). All effective character education programs have a clear vision of where they want to go, what they want to do, and why. This vision is made clear to all in a mission statement that is shared, used, and assessed.

A good model for a mission statement is that of the Mt. Lebanon School District (Pennsylvania), which has award-winning character education initiatives in place.

> *The mission of the Mt. Lebanon School District, as the leader of an educational partnership with the community, is to ensure that all students acquire the knowledge and skills to succeed and contribute as ethical, responsible citizens in a rapidly changing global society through a challenging, comprehensive program taught in a safe, caring environment by exceptional staff with continued involvement of families.*

> *We believe that the morally mature person habitually:*
> * *Respects human dignity.*
> * *Demonstrates active responsibility for the welfare of others.*
> * *Integrates individual interests and social responsibilities.*
> * *Demonstrates integrity.*
> * *Applies moral principles when making choices and judgments.*
> * *Seeks peaceful resolution of conflict.*

(See Readings: H. Huffman, p.51.)

The operative evaluation words in Mt. Lebanon's mission and values statements provide clues about what to assess:

- partnerships with the community and families
- knowledge and skills students need to prepare for further education and careers
- traits students need to become ethical, responsible citizens
- caring, safe, nurturing school environment
- comprehensive, challenging academic and character education program
- values of respect, honesty, responsibility, ethical decision making, conflict resolution, citizenship

Now that we have a model for your use, which can be called benchmarking, let's take the next step—how to evaluate your school's character education mission.

SES 2-1
Measuring the Mission

Edie Holcomb describes a way to monitor a school's mission using three key phrases: what we say (mission); evidence we have (what data shows the mission statement in action); and evidence we need (what data gives us a better picture of the mission statement in action). (See Readings: Holcomb, pp. 4-5.)

I have modified Holcomb's suggestions somewhat to meet the need for measuring your school's character education mission. These questions could be answered by the character education committee, but a better idea is to have stake holders complete the questions and then hold discussions on the answers and their implications. This process will enhance awareness and create action plans. Think of the richness and meaningfulness of conversations stake holders can have using these questions.

1. What do we say? (Our mission statement)

2. What are our operational words?

3. What do we know at this point?

4. What do we need to know?

5. What are we currently doing?

6. How well are we doing it?

7. What do we need to do?

8. What do we need to report to stake holders at this point?

9. What plans/actions do we need to take this school year?

10. What should our plans be for the next school year?

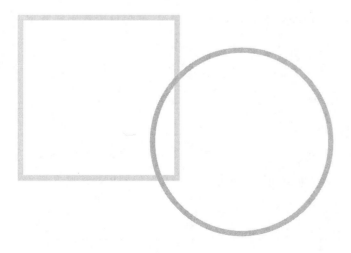

SES 2-2
Core Values— You Be the Judge

...We strongly urge each school district and community not to bypass or shortcut the process of defining its own values. By engaging in a process that is inclusive, students, school staff, and community members will develop a sense of ownership.... The result will be communities, schools, and students that are empowered to enforce the code, and are committed to practicing it.

The Commission for Ethical and Responsible Student Behavior (Maine Department of Education), Taking Responsibility.

This activity, conducted by the school's CEEC, can help stake holders identify and define the school's core values, if this has not been done earlier. Once the stake holders identify the core values, the committee needs to help them define each of the values. For example, if "respect" is listed as a core value, it needs to be defined operationally. That is, what does a respectful person do and not do? Or to put it another way, what do we expect of students, teachers, parents, and others who demonstrate the value of respect at our school.

IDENTIFICATION IS THE FIRST TASK, DEFINITION THE SECOND.

Schools that already have their core values defined should revisit them about every three to five years using an evaluation strategy like the one below. It may help to determine if stake holders wish to change the priority of their values or modify the definitions.

Values/Virtues/ Character Traits

Directions:
1. CIRCLE five values most important to you personally.
2. BLOCK those values that you want students to learn and practice in your school, school district, and community. (A few may not be those you circled.)
3. Meet with your group members (4-5 to a group) and try to reach CONSENSUS on 5 to 9 values. Write the consensus values in the space below.

Honesty	Integrity	Responsibility	Respect
Kindness	Cooperativeness	Courtesy	Patriotism
Loyalty	Justice	Tolerance	Patience
Golden Rule	Courage	Caring	Ambition
Trustworthiness	Compassion	Ethical Behavior	Fairness
Perseverance	Helpfulness	Courage	Self-discipline
Dependability	Love	Mercy	Unselfishness
Truthfulness	Reasonableness	Thrift	Obedience

Add others _____ _____ _____

_____ _____ _____ _____

**Small Group's
Consensus
Values**

1. _____
2. _____
3. _____
4. _____
5. _____
6. _____
7. _____
8. _____
9. _____

Have all small groups come together as one large group. One group places its values, one at a time, on the board or overhead, and each small group votes on whether that value was on their list. Each group gets one vote regardless of the number of members in that group. Repeat the process, with the second group placing its values that have not yet been shown for display. Only the values that get a majority vote stay on display. The values are that get the majority group vote are the ones that are to become part of the school's core values at least for the next year or so, when this process may be repeated.

**List the core
values selected.**

1. _____
2. _____
3. _____
4. _____
5. _____
6. _____
7. _____
8. _____
9. _____

NEXT TASK: DEFINE THE CORE VALUES SELECTED.

SES 2-3
Reflection

When we can't measure the things that are important, we ascribe importance to the things we can measure.

John Milton

Character Education Committee member: "Is there a short, quick way we can evaluate the effectiveness of our character education program?"

Ed: "Yes! Ask the bus drivers, playground supervisors, and substitute teachers."

Personal experience

Reflect on these two quotes, then discuss these questions:

1. How does the Milton quote relate to the accountability-testing thrust in your school?

2. Do you agree with Milton? Why, or why not?

3. What does the Milton quote have to say about character education in your school?

4. What is your response to the second quote?

5. What would substitute teachers say about "subbing" in your classroom?

6. What would your school's bus drivers, playground supervisors, and substitute teachers say about student behavior at your school? What about the respect and support they get from teachers, counselors and administrators?

Evaluating Character Development

SES 2-4
Focus Group—
The Ideal

Focus groups, although underused, provide an excellent qualitative evaluation process for assessing character education. Under the guidance of a moderator, small groups of people come together to have conversations about very specific questions regarding the school's character education efforts. For example, wouldn't it be of interest to have students from various grade levels discuss their opinions and experiences in the program?

How helpful would it be to have teacher focus groups meet to discuss the issues of staff development, resources, or for that matter, the selection of a commercial character education program? Here are some strategies the committee should use when planning focus groups.

- Identify the questions to be asked of the groups. The same questions may be asked of several different groups. Decide on how many focus-group sessions will be held and when.

- Select a moderator. A professional moderator will keep the discussions on point, but it's an extra cost you might not be able to afford. I suggest looking for a person in the school district with a reputation of working well with groups. The moderator should be someone who does not work in your school. Thus the moderator will have greater objectivity and participants will be encouraged to open up more on issues or concerns.

- Be sure the moderator has a committee-approved agenda in the form of questions to be asked.

- Don't mix the participants; that is, do not have focus groups that mix teachers with administrators, students with teachers, parents with students. Focus group members need equal status and common experiences.

- Select a meeting area that is comfortable, and limit sessions to about ninety minutes.

- Decide if observers (note-takers) will be used. If so, inform the participants when they are invited to participate in the focus group. Tell them why observers are in the room. Limit observers to one or two people.

- After a focus-group session, ask the moderator and observer(s) to write up a description of what they heard and submit their report (maybe five pages that focused on the questions) to the committee.

Dean, D. "How to Use Focus Groups." In *Handbook of Practical Program Evaluation*. Joseph S. Wholey, Harry P. Hatry, and Kathryn E. Newcomer, eds., San Francisco: Jossey-Bass Publishers, 1994.)

Questions to be discussed in first hour of the focus-group sessions:
- What might a school look like that is based on a set of core values such as caring, respect, responsibility, and trust?
- What would a school be like that had a reputation for being a caring, civil, and collegial place to teach and learn?

Another set of questions:

- Describe how students behave when they demonstrate such traits as respect and responsibility.

- What are the factors that make teachers and students look forward to coming to school each day?

Question for the last half-hour of this focus-group session:

- How do the answers to the above questions inform your group about the mission and values of this school?

Evaluating Character Development

Section 3	# Expectations and Outcomes

In its broadest sense, the word outcomes, in the context of evaluation, means determining the expectations stake holders have for the school's character education efforts and the student behaviors they are looking for. It means that stake holders meet head on the following questions:

- Why do we want a character education program?
- What do we want this school's character education mission to be?
- What are our programmatic expectations?
- What changes in the school culture do we want?
- What outcomes do we desire?
- What do we expect of our students and their parents?
- What expectations do we have for school personnel?
- Do we have expectations for community agencies, institutions, organizations, groups, and individuals?

These and other questions will guide stake holders' evaluation efforts. They will serve as reference points throughout the evaluation process, and they will be the benchmarks against which character education efforts will be compared.

In this section of the framework, we will look at outcomes through several lenses. The sample evaluation strategies will ask stake holders about school climate and student behaviors. Their perceptions will be solicited, and recommendations for establishing baseline data will be offered. The CEEC should also examine the instruments and readings recommended at the end of this book as the committee attempts to assess the impact of the school's character education initiatives on school climate and student behaviors.

SES 3-1
School Outcomes

Respondent:

☐ Teacher   ☐ Administrator   ☐ Student
☐ Support Staff   ☐ Parent   ☐ Central Office Administrator
☐ Community Partner   ☐ Other _____

Directions: Since this school has implemented a character education program, what improvements have you seen or experienced? Use this scale:

5 = Major Improvement   **4 = Considerable Improvement**
3 = Some Improvement   **2 = Minimal Improvement**
1 = No Improvement

1. The school's image and reputation	5	4	3	2	1
2. Relationships among school personnel	5	4	3	2	1
3. Relationships between teachers and students	5	4	3	2	1
4. Shared decision making	5	4	3	2	1
5. A safer environment	5	4	3	2	1
6. Fewer classroom interruptions	5	4	3	2	1
7. More parent involvement	5	4	3	2	1
8. Better school partnerships	5	4	3	2	1
9. Better relationships among the students	5	4	3	2	1
10. Greater attention to the school's core values	5	4	3	2	1
11. More civil and polite language	5	4	3	2	1
12. More support from the school's administrators	5	4	3	2	1

What has impressed you MOST about this school's character education efforts?

_____

_____

What still needs to be done?

_____

_____

What is the reputation of the school in this community?

_____

_____

What do you like or not like about this school?

_____

_____

SES 3-2
Student Outcomes

Respondent:

☐ Teacher   ☐ Administrator   ☐ Student

☐ Support Staff   ☐ Parent   ☐ Central Office Administrator

☐ Community Partner   ☐ Other _____

Directions: Using the following 20 items below, please answer the question that follows. Check one space for each item.

What has happened to students since the implementation of this school's character education program?

1. Their behavior has
   ☐ greatly improved   ☐ improved somewhat   ☐ not improved.

2. The dropout rate has
   ☐ increased   ☐ decreased   ☐ stayed about the same.

3. Their attendance rate has
   ☐ increased   ☐ decreased   ☐ stayed about the same.

4. Their attitudes have
   ☐ improved greatly   ☐ improved modestly   ☐ not improved.

5. Their service/volunteering has
   ☐ increased   ☐ decreased   ☐ not changed.

6. Their use of civil language has
   ☐ greatly improved   ☐ improved modestly   ☐ not changed.

7. Their participation in the school's activities programs (sports, clubs, etc.) has
   ☐ increased   ☐ decreased   ☐ not changed.

8. Their academic achievement has
   ☐ greatly improved   ☐ improved somewhat   ☐ not changed.

9. Their motivation to do school work has
   ☐ greatly improved   ☐ improved somewhat   ☐ not changed.

10. Incidences of student physical violence have
    ☐ increased   ☐ decreased   ☐ not changed.

11. Incidences of student verbal abuse (bullying, ridiculing, blaming, angering, tormenting, etc.) have
    ☐ greatly decreased   ☐ decreased somewhat   ☐ not improved.

12. Their involvement in school affairs (rules, policies, taking leadership roles) has
    ☐ increased significantly   ☐ increased somewhat   ☐ not changed.

13. Student relationships with teachers have
    ☐ greatly improved   ☐ improved somewhat   ☐ not changed.

14. Student attentiveness in class has
    ☐ greatly improved   ☐ improved somewhat   ☐ not improved that much.

15. Students seem to be
    ☐ more respectful   ☐ less respectful   ☐ about the same.

16. The relationships among students seems to have
    ☐ improved dramatically   ☐ improved modestly   ☐ not changed.

17. Their participation in cooperative learning activities (group work, teamwork) has
    ☐ greatly improved   ☐ improved modestly   ☐ not improved.

18. Students' critical thinking skills have
    ☐ really improved   ☐ improved somewhat   ☐ not improved.

19. Their knowledge about the school's core values is
    ☐ impressive   ☐ better   ☐ minimal.

20. Their application of the school's core values is
    ☐ heartwarming   ☐ not as good as it should be
    ☐ leaves much to be desired.

SES 3-3

School Climate: Attitude Scale

Measuring school climate can help us understand what was and what is, so that we can move forward to what could be.

H. Jerome Freiberg, "Measuring School Climate: Let Me Count the Ways." *Educational Leadership*

Strong, positive cultures are places with a shared sense of what is important, a shared ethos of caring and concern, and a shared commitment to helping students learn....

Ken Peterson and Terence Deal, "How Leaders Influence the Culture of Schools." *Educational Leadership*

There are many instruments available for assessing school climate or culture. The focus in this one is on a school's climate as it relates to the school's character education efforts. Many of the items are based on the findings and recommendations of James Leming's research work reported in *Character Education: Lessons from the Past, Models for the Future* (Camden, Me.: Institute for Global Ethics, 1993.)

The character education committee may administer this instrument to different stake holder groups at different times. For example, the first time the instrument is used, the committee may wish to survey only the students, and later only the parents. This will depend on the time and resources available to collate, analyze and report the information gleaned from this scale. Remember that climate is to a school what character is to an individual.

Respondent:

☐ Teacher ☐ Administrator ☐ Student
☐ Support Staff ☐ Parent ☐ Central Office Administrator
☐ Community Partner ☐ Other _____

Directions: After each statement, circle the number indicating the extent to which you agree or disagree.

5 = Strongly agree   **4 = Agree**   **3 = Neutral**
2 = Disagree   **1= Strongly disagree**

5	4	3	2	1	1. This school is a safe place to be.
5	4	3	2	1	2. School rules are clear and fairly applied.
5	4	3	2	1	3. Standards for student achievement are clear.
5	4	3	2	1	4. Standards for student behavior are clear.
5	4	3	2	1	5. There is mutual respect between teachers and students.
5	4	3	2	1	6. This school is free from bullying and harassment.
5	4	3	2	1	7. Students respect each other in this school.
5	4	3	2	1	8. Core values are modeled by adults in this school.
5	4	3	2	1	9. Cooperative teaching and learning strategies are used in most of the classes.
5	4	3	2	1	10. Students are really engaged in this school's character education efforts.

5	4	3	2	1	11. Communication is a real problem in this school.
5	4	3	2	1	12. There are high expectations for positive student behavior.
5	4	3	2	1	13. Most classes are orderly and free of disruptions.
5	4	3	2	1	14. In this school you will find most of us using civil, positive language.
5	4	3	2	1	15. Our school's character education efforts involve parents.
5	4	3	2	1	16. This community supports the work we do to teach, learn, and practice the core values.
5	4	3	2	1	17. The cafeteria is a safe and pleasant place to eat.
5	4	3	2	1	18. There is respect for the property of others.
5	4	3	2	1	19. You won't find graffiti at this school.
					20. Add other items.

5 4 3 2 1   _____

_____

5 4 3 2 1   _____

_____

5 4 3 2 1   _____

_____

SES 3-4
School Climate: Perception Checklist

In this second instrument for assessing school climate as it relates to the school's character education efforts, respondents' perceptions are captured in the words they might use to characterize the climate of the school. Many of the words may represent the school's core values.

Respondent:

☐ Teacher ☐ Administrator ☐ Student
☐ Support Staff ☐ Parent ☐ Central Office Administrator
☐ Community Partner ☐ Other _____

Directions: Place a check mark at the point between the two words that represents how you feel about this school.

1. Caring ____ ____ ____ ____ ____ Uncaring
2. Civil ____ ____ ____ ____ ____ Uncivil
3. Safe ____ ____ ____ ____ ____ Unsafe
4. Warm ____ ____ ____ ____ ____ Cold
5. Fair ____ ____ ____ ____ ____ Unfair
6. Respectful ____ ____ ____ ____ ____ Disrespectful
7. Responsible ____ ____ ____ ____ ____ Irresponsible
8. Exciting ____ ____ ____ ____ ____ Dull
9. Honest ____ ____ ____ ____ ____ Dishonest
10. Good ____ ____ ____ ____ ____ Bad
11. Tolerant ____ ____ ____ ____ ____ Intolerant
12. Flexible ____ ____ ____ ____ ____ Rigid
13. Democratic ____ ____ ____ ____ ____ Authoritarian
14. Courteous ____ ____ ____ ____ ____ Discourteous
15. Supportive ____ ____ ____ ____ ____ Nonsupportive

Select five of the words above that best describes this school's character education efforts. Write them here:

_____
_____
_____
_____
_____

SES 3-5
Baseline Data Behavior Scale

In Part I of this book, the suggestion was made that the school's character education evaluation committee become data savvy, that is, establish baseline data that will help quantify some of the effects of the school's character education efforts. Two questions are being addressed here:

1. Have our character education efforts had any impact on students' misbehaviors? (See vandalism example that follows.)

2. Does the data identify the need for additional school-wide intervention programs?

In most cases, it would be more interesting to have these data before the school's character education initiatives begin, but experience suggests that collecting such data comes as a result of the committee's first-year experiences leading the school's efforts. In any event, data are useful and informative, and should be gathered as early as possible after program implementation.

There is much hard data floating around a school regarding student behavior. You can probably find abundant statistics about classroom disruptions, vandalism, harassment, violence, attendance, expulsions, suspensions, racial/ethnic incidents, thefts, property damage, cheating, bullying, drug/alcohol use, smoking, and disciplinary referrals.

A data-collection pattern is outlined below. The committee should define the meaning of high, average, and low achievement, absentee and truancy rates, as well as discipline referrals for their school. The assumption here is the school's character education evaluation committee will ask the administration to collect data for the "behavior factor" to be examined. The intent is to look for changes or trends over the school year and then to compare data for each succeeding school year. The committee's view about data collection should be: Collect it—Examine it—Share it—Use it!

Below is an example of data collection for one behavior factor. It can also be used to collect data on violence, cheating, theft, etc.

Vandalism

School year_____   Person/group collecting data_____

Time of year data collected/examined   ☐ Fall   ☐ Winter   ☐ Spring

Number of recorded incidents   _____

Number of students identified   _____

Number of incidents by an individual student   _____

Percent of incidents by gender   M_____   F_____

Percent of incidents by class/grade   F_____ S_____ J_____ S _____

Percent of incidents by students with HIGH achievement   _____
                                       AVERAGE achievement   _____
                                            LOW achievement   _____

Percent of incidents by students with HIGH absentee rates   _____
                                       AVERAGE absentee rates   _____
                                            LOW absentee rates   _____

Percent of incidents by students with truancy rates that are

      HIGH _____   AVERAGE _____   LOW _____

Percent of incidents by students with disciplinary referrals that are

      HIGH _____   AVERAGE _____   LOW _____

Percent of incidents by students identified with gangs   _____

Percent of incidents by students who have

  TWO suspensions _____   FOUR suspensions _____

  SIX + suspensions _____

Other factors may be listed here so that there is a clear picture of the rate of vandalism occurring in or on the school property.

_____

_____

_____

_____

_____

_____

_____

_____

_____

_____

_____

_____

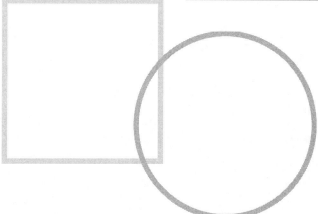

SES 3-6
Student Self-Evaluation Inventory

This form is a way for you to examine some of your behaviors as part of this school's efforts to nurture the core values (identify them here). It is designed to help you think about some very important social skills. You do not have to turn it in. We will have a class discussion about your reactions to the items on this form.

Directions: According to the scale below, how would others rate you and how would you rate yourself? Record your responses on the lines provided.

A = all the time   B = most of the time
C = some of the time   D = seldom or never

Do you/Are You... *As rated by:*	You	Friends	Teacher(s)	Parents
Think before acting	_____	_____	_____	_____
Respectful	_____	_____	_____	_____
Trustworthy	_____	_____	_____	_____
Control your temper	_____	_____	_____	_____
Caring and helpful	_____	_____	_____	_____
Stay out of fights	_____	_____	_____	_____
A good listener	_____	_____	_____	_____
Takes responsibility for actions	_____	_____	_____	_____
Deals with own anger	_____	_____	_____	_____
Use civil language	_____	_____	_____	_____
Can handle peer pressure	_____	_____	_____	_____
Honest	_____	_____	_____	_____
Seek peaceful solution to conflicts	_____	_____	_____	_____
A good group member	_____	_____	_____	_____
Avoid at-risk behaviors	_____	_____	_____	_____
Stand up for own/others' rights	_____	_____	_____	_____

SES 3-7
Students' Prosocial Behaviors Perception Scale

Respondent:

☐ Teacher ☐ Student ☐ Administrator
☐ School Staff ☐ Parent ☐ Other _____

Directions: Answer the question below using this scale:

Most = 70% or more   Many = 50-69%
Some = 30-49%   Few = 30% or less

Since this school has implemented a character education program, how many students now exhibit/demonstrate/practice the following prosocial/proactive behaviors?

More respectful?	☐ most	☐ many	☐ some	☐ few
More responsible?	☐ most	☐ many	☐ some	☐ few
More caring?	☐ most	☐ many	☐ some	☐ few
More cooperative?	☐ most	☐ many	☐ some	☐ few
Kinder?	☐ most	☐ many	☐ some	☐ few
Show less at-risk behavior?	☐ most	☐ many	☐ some	☐ few
Less lonely or isolated?	☐ most	☐ many	☐ some	☐ few
More engaged in class work?	☐ most	☐ many	☐ some	☐ few
More interested in taking leadership responsibilities?	☐ most	☐ many	☐ some	☐ few
More willing to reach peaceful resolution to conflicts?	☐ most	☐ many	☐ some	☐ few
More positive relationship among students?	☐ most	☐ many	☐ some	☐ few
Greater willingness to help others?	☐ most	☐ many	☐ some	☐ few
More interested in school work?	☐ most	☐ many	☐ some	☐ few
Greater appreciation of each other's differences?	☐ most	☐ many	☐ some	☐ few
Greater enjoyment in school activities?	☐ most	☐ many	☐ some	☐ few
More ethical?	☐ most	☐ many	☐ some	☐ few
Greater interest in community affairs?	☐ most	☐ many	☐ some	☐ few
Less substance abuse?	☐ most	☐ many	☐ some	☐ few
More student volunteers at school and in community?	☐ most	☐ many	☐ some	☐ few
More willing to confront bullies?	☐ most	☐ many	☐ some	☐ few

Is this school a better place to teach and learn than it was before the school's character education instruction was implemented?

_____
_____
_____
_____

How would you rate the school culture since the implementation of character education efforts?

_____
_____
_____
_____

How should the school culture be improved?

_____
_____
_____
_____

Why is it better than before, or why is it no better than before?

_____
_____
_____
_____

Please return this form to a member of CEEC or the school secretary. Your name is not necessary.

SES 3-8
At-Risk Behavior Perception Scale

Respondent:

☐ Teacher   ☐ Student (grade: _____)   ☐ male   ☐ female)

☐ Administrator   ☐ School Staff   ☐ Parent

Directions: Using the scale below, circle the number that best represents your opinions about the extent to which these negative behaviors exist in this school, classroom, or off school grounds.

5 = great extent   4 = some extent

3 = very little   2 = not at all

Behaviors	In school	In classroom	On playground	On school bus
Bullying	5 4 3 2	5 4 3 2	5 4 3 2	5 4 3 2
Fighting	5 4 3 2	5 4 3 2	5 4 3 2	5 4 3 2
Stealing	5 4 3 2	5 4 3 2	5 4 3 2	5 4 3 2
Vandalism	5 4 3 2	5 4 3 2	5 4 3 2	5 4 3 2
Substance Abuse	5 4 3 2	5 4 3 2	5 4 3 2	5 4 3 2
Punching/Hitting	5 4 3 2	5 4 3 2	5 4 3 2	5 4 3 2
Cursing	5 4 3 2	5 4 3 2	5 4 3 2	5 4 3 2
Pushing/Slapping	5 4 3 2	5 4 3 2	5 4 3 2	5 4 3 2
Taunting/Tormenting/ Teasing	5 4 3 2	5 4 3 2	5 4 3 2	5 4 3 2
Threatening	5 4 3 2	5 4 3 2	5 4 3 2	5 4 3 2
Blaming/Condemning	5 4 3 2	5 4 3 2	5 4 3 2	5 4 3 2
Ridiculing/Insulting	5 4 3 2	5 4 3 2	5 4 3 2	5 4 3 2
Lying	5 4 3 2	5 4 3 2	5 4 3 2	5 4 3 2
Name Calling	5 4 3 2	5 4 3 2	5 4 3 2	5 4 3 2
Specify Other:	5 4 3 2	5 4 3 2	5 4 3 2	5 4 3 2

_____

SES 3-9
Student Integrity Questionnaire

This sample evaluation questionnaire might be used to gather additional baseline data about student integrity (honesty, cheating, etc.). Depending on the results, it may help focus some of the content/lessons in your school's character education program.

The instrument not only helps the character education evaluation committee (CEEC) gather data, it also informs the students that there is interest by teachers and administrators in such behaviors. For example, in a three-year middle school, first-year students might complete the questionnaire near the end of the year, and then again during their second and third years at the school. At a high school, the questionnaire might be given to a sampling of the freshman class and administered each year as the class progresses through the next three years.

Comparing the findings might be informative and instructive. The CEEC can add any variables they are interested in examining (e.g., gender or achievement level).

This student-integrity questionnaire was brought to my attention by Claire Patin, a character education specialist and math teacher at Francis Parker School (San Diego). It was written for the school by Deborah Bright, an English teacher at "Parker," and has been modified for the purposes of this book with permission from the author.

Directions: Please answer the following questions honestly and openly. Your answers will help us track behaviors that we hope will inform our work in this school's character education program. Place a check mark in the appropriate space following each item. Your name is not necessary.

(Note: CEEC would place demographic data request here.)

HOW OFTEN HAVE YOU...

	Never	A few times	Many times
1. copied someone else's homework?	☐	☐	☐
2. copied off of a web site?	☐	☐	☐
3. let someone copy your homework?	☐	☐	☐
4. let someone copy off you during a quiz or test?	☐	☐	☐
5. copied off someone during a quiz or test?	☐	☐	☐
6. let your parents/family member/tutor or friend do more of your homework than you knew to be appropriate?	☐	☐	☐
7. gotten questions or answers (e.g., between classes) to a quiz or test?	☐	☐	☐
8. used notes/crib sheets during a test/quiz?	☐	☐	☐
9. given someone questions or answers from a test or quiz?	☐	☐	☐
10. missed part or all of a school day because you were unprepared for a test or an assignment?	☐	☐	☐

ARE YOU AWARE OF ANY OF YOUR FRIENDS OR CLASSMATES WHO...

11. copy other students' homework?   ☐ YES   ☐ NO

12. allow parents/family members/tutor or friends do more of their homework than was appropriate?   ☐ YES   ☐ NO

13. get answers to tests or quizzes?   ☐ YES   ☐ NO

14. cheat during a test or quiz?   ☐ YES   ☐ NO

15. copy from someone else's test or quiz?   ☐ YES   ☐ NO

16. copy website information and use it as their own work?   ☐ YES   ☐ NO

17. missed part or all of a school day because they were unprepared for a test or an assignment?   ☐ YES   ☐ NO

IF YOU KNEW SOMEONE...

18. who was cheating in any way, would you (check all that apply)
    - ☐ talk to him/her about it suggesting he/she stop
    - ☐ tell a teacher
    - ☐ tell a friend
    - ☐ tell a parent
    - ☐ do nothing
    - ☐ do something but it depends on who it is
    - ☐ other options (list one) _____

19. who makes racist or bigoted remarks, would you (check all that apply)
    - ☐ talk to him/her as the remarks are being said about how you feel
    - ☐ ignore it, do nothing
    - ☐ simply walk away and let the person continue
    - ☐ tell someone else how bad such remarks make you feel
    - ☐ get advice from your parents on how to handle such a situation
    - ☐ get advice from a teacher or counselor
    - ☐ ask a friend how best to handle it
    - ☐ other options (list one) _____

20. who had used drugs or alcohol, or had an eating disorder, or stole things, or cheated, would you (check all that apply)
    - ☐ talk to him/her and express you concerns
    - ☐ talk to him/her and insist that he/she seek help
    - ☐ tell his/her parents
    - ☐ ask your parents for advice
    - ☐ tell a teacher or counselor
    - ☐ do nothing because it's not your business
    - ☐ tell some friends so that together you can do something
    - ☐ other options (list one) _____

Please indicate whether or not you think each of the following statements is true or false by circling T or F.

21. Lying is a relative thing; it depends on the situation. T F

22. A person who lies often enough in "insignificant situations," may also lie in important situations. T F

23. The ends justify the means; that is, as long as the result is what you want, it doesn't matter how you get it. T T

24. Cheating is a relative thing. It really depends on how big the "stakes" are (e.g., a quiz vs. a major test). T F

25. Because of parent pressure, most students at this school go after high grades no matter what the cost. T F

26. Because of the pressure to get into the "right" college or university, many students at this school will cheat/lie/plagiarize to get good grades. T F

Please answer these questions.

27. How much of a problem is cheating at this school?

_____
_____
_____

28. How much of a problem is stealing at this school?

_____
_____
_____

29. If there is a problem with cheating or lying in test-taking and/or doing assignments, whose fault is it?

_____
_____
_____

30. What is your greatest concern about going to this school?

_____
_____
_____

| Section 4 | # Curriculum and Programs |

The hallmark of a successful organization is a shared sense among its members about what they are trying to accomplish. Agreed-upon goals and ways to attain them enhance the organization's capacity for rational planning and action.

Susan Rosenholtz, *Teacher's Workplace: The Social Organization of Schools*

Consider a school where teachers know exactly what essential skills and knowledge students should learn that year and where they know that their colleagues are teaching to the same manageable standards.

Mike Schmoker & Robert Marzano, "Realizing the Promise of Standards-based Education." *Educational Leadership*

Imagine this scenario in your school. Everyone knows why there is a character education program. Everyone is working collaboratively to accomplish its goals. Stake holders are actively and cooperatively engaged in developing and implementing programs that promote the core virtues and other aspects of the character education program. Consider the appropriateness of program standards that can guide such efforts.

Before looking at a program-standard evaluation checklist, it is necessary to define program. In this checklist, program means the curriculum, co-curriculum, units, lessons, the virtue-a-month plan, service learning, and teachable moments. It includes school-wide activities such as assemblies and celebrations. Parent and community programs are part of the definition, as are commercial programs and intervention programs.

SES 4-1

Program Standards Checklist

Respondent:

☐ Administrator   ☐ Teacher   ☐ Committee member

Directions: Please determine the extent to which your school's character education efforts are in compliance with the standard statement, using numbers on this continuum. Write the number after each item.

5	4	3	2	1
Compliance		Moderate compliance		Noncompliance

UK = Unknown

Our school's character education program...

Score

1. fosters and enhances the school's core virtues. _____

2. is guided by a mission and goals. _____

3. has a specific set of expectations and outcomes. _____

4. engages parents in this school's character education efforts. _____

5. enables students to take leadership roles. _____

6. offers school personnel staff development opportunities. _____

7. is aligned with strategies for program and personnel evaluation _____

8. utilizes intervention methods to solve specific problems (e.g., violence). _____

9. is effectively communicated to all stake holders. _____

10. uses commercial programs that meet the program's mission and goals. _____

11. builds positive relationships among the stake holders. _____

12. contributes to the moral and social development of all students. _____

13. is assessed on a regular basis to determine what works and what doesn't. _____

14. improves the quality of life in this school. _____

15. contributes to a positive school climate. _____

16. is based on best practices and research findings. _____

17. is integrated into both the regular curriculum and co-curricular programs. _____

18. values the many multicultural traditions of students and their families. _____

19. balances knowledge acquisition with practice. _____

20. promotes students' critical thinking and moral reasoning skills. _____

21. offers students in-school and community service learning opportunities. _____

22. provides teachers and students with the resources needed for instruction. _____

23. Other _____ _____

A. List the numbers of all items not in compliance here.

_____

_____

_____

_____

B. Describe discrepancies/evidence that causes a score of 3 or less:

_____

_____

_____

_____

C. Identify actions needed to reach compliance.

_____

_____

_____

_____

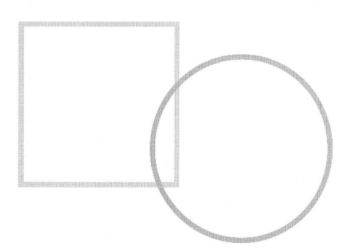

SES 4-2
Character Education Activities: Use Scale

Here's an example of where the items on the instrument can be used both to educate personnel who complete the instrument and as an evaluation tool to assess recommended activities/programs found in many award-winning schools.

The purpose of this scale is to help the school's character education committee estimate the extent to which the following character development activities/programs/strategies are being used by teachers and others. A second purpose is to determine respondents' interest in learning more about the topic identified in each item.

Respondent:
☐ Teacher   ☐ Administrator
☐ Supervisor   ☐ Other_____

Directions: To what extent is the activity/program/strategy used in our character education efforts? Using the following scale, circle the number that best expresses your opinion.

1 = to a great extent   2 = to some extent   3 = not used at all

Next, circle the letter that tells us what you know about the item/topic.

A = know enough about this
B = need to know more about this
C = Not interested

1.	Cooperative learning	1	2	3	A	B	C
2.	Service learning	1	2	3	A	B	C
3.	Trait-of-the-month program	1	2	3	A	B	C
4.	Posters/banners/bulletin boards	1	2	3	A	B	C
5.	Literature-based program	1	2	3	A	B	C
6.	Rewards/recognition programs	1	2	3	A	B	C
7.	Direct teaching of values	1	2	3	A	B	C
8.	Co-curricular program	1	2	3	A	B	C
9.	Student activities program	1	2	3	A	B	C
10.	Conflict resolution	1	2	3	A	B	C
11.	Violence-prevention program	1	2	3	A	B	C
12.	Peer mediation	1	2	3	A	B	C
13.	Problem-centered learning	1	2	3	A	B	C
14.	Staff development opportunities	1	2	3	A	B	C
15.	Parent involvement activities	1	2	3	A	B	C
16.	Community support activities	1	2	3	A	B	C
17.	Critical thinking emphasis	1	2	3	A	B	C
18.	Discipline policies/activities	1	2	3	A	B	C
19.	Substance-abuse program	1	2	3	A	B	C
20.	Class meetings	1	2	3	A	B	C
21.	Activities that focus on core values	1	2	3	A	B	C
22.	Use of teachable moments	1	2	3	A	B	C

For items that you circled a 3, why, in your opinion, is this activity/program/ strategy not part of the school's character education efforts?

_____

_____

_____

_____

For any item where you circled C, tell us why you are not interested.

_____

_____

_____

_____

SES 4-3
Service Learning: Teachers' Perceptions

The fact is that students benefit both academically and socially from an education that integrates challenging academics with a commitment to creating a caring and civil community. This is not an either/or choice.... We can not only enrich our academic content but also nurture an ethic of care and service in young people.

Sheldon Berman, Superintendent, Hudson Public Schools (Massachusetts)

Character education without service learning is like baseball practice without a game. A recent survey reported that about one-third of all public schools and half of all public high schools provided some form of service learning for all students. Research shows that service learning positively affects students' personal development while helping them become more knowledgeable about careers, and enhances their respect for teachers and other students. It also improves the school culture and leads to more positive perceptions of schools and youth by community members. (Billig, S. Service Learning Impacts on Youth, Schools, and Community: Research on K-12 School-Based Service Learning,1990-1999. Denver, Colo.: RMC Research Corporation, 2000.)

Service learning (SL) in most schools is some combination of community projects, in-school projects, student-club-related and student-initiated projects, and curriculum-based projects and activities. As such, much can and should be evaluated regarding the service learning program at your school. Ongoing (formative) evaluation is essential to determine program effectiveness, staff development needs, and resource allocations. Summative evaluation plans should be designed to determine program impact on the school, students, stake holders, and the community.

Two evaluation strategies, useful to the school's character education evaluation committee, include a teachers' perception scale and an impact questionnaire.

Grade level _____ or Subjects you teach_____

Participation in Service Learning   ☐ A lot   ☐ Some   ☐ None

Directions: Circle the response that best describes the extent to which you agree or disagree with each statement.

SA = strongly agree   **A = agree**   **N = neutral**
D = disagree   **SD = strongly disagree**

SA   A   N   D   SD   1. This school's service learning program is an integral part of the school's character education program.

SA   A   N   D   SD   2. In most cases, teachers link service learning with content and course standards.

SA   A   N   D   SD   3. Service learning is taking too much time from the content I am responsible to teach.

SA   A   N   D   SD   4. Service learning helps students learn the meaning and relevancy of what they are being taught.

SA   A   N   D   SD   5. The school's core values can be learned just as well without spending all this time on service learning.

SA   A   N   D   SD   6. Service learning has helped teachers in this school engage in team efforts.

SA   A   N   D   SD   7. Service learning, like the school's core values, is well integrated into the curriculum.

SA   A   N   D   SD   8. The staff uses service learning opportunities to help students enhance their leadership and citizenship skills.

SA   A   N   D   SD   9. Service learning helps us teachers be more creative and innovative in our teaching.

SA   A   N   D   SD   10. Service learning helps teachers promote cross-disciplinary activities for students.

What comments/recommendations would you like to share with our CEEC?

_____
_____
_____
_____
_____
_____

SES 4-4
Service Learning: Impact Questionnaire

Respondent:

☐ Teacher   ☐ Administrator   ☐ Coordinator   ☐ Parent
☐ Community member   ☐ Other (specify) _____

Directions: Please answer the following questions as best as you can. If you do not have enough information, indicate with UK=unknown. Feel free to share your opinions with us even though your information may be limited.

What is the impact of the service-learning component on the school's character education initiatives?

A. SCHOOL CULTURE—Has it changed for the better?

_____

_____

B. CLASSROOM CLIMATE—Has it become more civil and caring?

_____

_____

C. COMMUNITY—Do recipients of service learning have more favorable views of the school and the students?

_____

_____

D. PARENTS—Have parents seen any behavioral changes in their sons/daughters as a result of participating in service learning? Do parents take an active role in the program?

_____

_____

E. CURRICULUM—Has service learning been infused throughout the curriculum including the co-curricular offerings?

_____

_____

F. INSTRUCTION—Has service-learning instruction capitalized on students as resources and learners responsible for their own learning? Has it resulted in the concept of teacher as facilitator, in team teaching, and in creating a community of learners?

_____

_____

_____

G. STUDENTS—Has service learning had any effect on students'...

• academic achievement? _____

• citizenship skills? _____

• sense of civic responsibility? _____

• demonstration of school's core values? _____

• ability to reflect on experiences orally and in writing
  or in some other creative way? _____

• attendance at school? _____

• time-management skills? _____

• attitude towards others? _____

• self-esteem, self-worth? _____

• responsibility for their own learning? _____

• appreciation for teamwork and collaboration? _____

• awareness of the needs of others at school
  and in the community? _____

• other (specify) _____

SES 4-5
Meeting Student's Needs: Evaluation Form

Respondent:

☐ Teacher   ☐ Administrator

☐ Counselor   ☐ Student

Directions: Using the scale below, rate how you feel this school's character education programs meet the social-behavioral needs of students. "Programs" include all planned activities designed to help students develop good character. Some examples are the school's core virtues, lessons, units, themes, school-wide activities, community projects, service learning, and the like. Circle the number that best applies.

Scale: 0 = does not apply

1 = no opinion

2 = program definitely meets this need

3 = program sometimes meets this need

4 = program seldom meets this need

5 = program never meets this need

THE NEED TO...

0	1	2	3	4	5	1. understand responsibilities of living in a democracy.
0	1	2	3	4	5	2. be responsible for own behavior.
0	1	2	3	4	5	3. learn and practice good character.
0	1	2	3	4	5	4. live and work cooperatively with others.
0	1	2	3	4	5	5. resolve conflicts peacefully.
0	1	2	3	4	5	6. think before acting/doing.
0	1	2	3	4	5	7. care about the welfare of others.
0	1	2	3	4	5	8. think and act morally.
0	1	2	3	4	5	9. manage one's emotions.
0	1	2	3	4	5	10. be respectful.
0	1	2	3	4	5	11. use civil language.
0	1	2	3	4	5	12. deal with failure or embarrassment.
0	1	2	3	4	5	13. appreciate the importance of physical and mental health.
0	1	2	3	4	5	14. appreciate people of all races, ethnicities, and creeds.
0	1	2	3	4	5	15. treat others with equal respect.

Add other needs here

0	1	2	3	4	5	16. _____
0	1	2	3	4	5	17. _____

Share with the committee any comments that will help us evaluate our character education efforts.

_____

_____

_____

SES 4-6
Evaluating Character Education Activities (Assemblies)

There are many school-wide activities that are part of the school's character education efforts. Award-winning schools often feature activities such as awards events, assemblies, guest speakers, class meetings, parent resource centers, principal's morning "value" announcements, poster and banner displays, peer mediation, buddies activities, daily television programs, multicultural luncheons, student clubs and councils.

This strategy evaluates students' views of school assemblies that are designed to foster the school's core values and contribute to the character development of students. This survey of assemblies can easily be adapted to evaluate other school-wide activities merely by substituting another activity and modifying the statement.

Dear Student,

The Character Education Evaluation Committee is interested in your views of this year's assemblies that focused on the school's character education program and the core values. Please complete the statement below stating the extent to which you agree or disagree with the statement. Circle one of the following after each item:

SA = strongly agree   **A = agree**   **N = neutral**
D = disagree   **SD = strongly disagree**   **DK = don't know**

Your answers to the questions 10 and 11 are especially important to us. Return this survey form to your teacher. Your name is not necessary.

SA A N D SD DK   1. The assemblies on values and character were a waste of time.

SA A N D SD DK   2. The assemblies made me more aware of the school's core values.

SA A N D SD DK   3. I am more motivated to practice and use the core values because of the assemblies.

SA A N D SD DK   4. I like them, they were a good break from the work in class.

SA A N D SD DK   5. Seeing and hearing people speak about how the core values influenced their lives was inspiring to me.

SA A N D SD DK   6. Students are involved in preparing and conducting our school's "values assemblies."

SA A N D SD DK   7. I hear my classmates discussing what they have heard and learned at these assemblies.

SA A N D SD DK   8. Teachers seldom talk about the "character trait/value assemblies" when we get back to the classroom.

SA A N D SD DK   9. Students like to go to assemblies because it give us a sense of school spirit.

SA A N D SD DK   10. Have would you use the values discussed at the assemblies at home and at school?

_____

_____

11. What suggestions do you have for improving the assemblies that address the school's character education program and core values?

_____

_____

Note: My thanks to three teachers—Claire Patin, Carla Berk, and Michele Gallo—for the original idea and a sample form which I have adapted to create this survey instrument.

SES 4-7
Students' Reflection Scale: Responsibility

Most schools have some kind of an organizational plan for integrating the school's core values into the curriculum and teachers' instructional plans. The most popular method is the value-a-month program (VAMP). Here is an example:

FRESNO UNIFIED SCHOOL DISTRICT (CA)

SEPTEMBER = Helping others	FEBRUARY = Respect
OCTOBER = Responsibility	MARCH = Self-worth
NOVEMBER = Freedom	APRIL = Loyalty
DECEMBER = Love	MAY = Justice
JANUARY = Integrity	

VAMP is a framework that helps teachers and administrators focus on each of the school's core values in the daily curriculum, school-wide activities, and special projects. Teachers report that it is of great help to them in their planning and instruction on values. Many schools tie it into some of the monthly themes of the calendar. For example, in September the value of the month might be related to celebrations and themes, such as Back-To-School Month, National Childhood Injury Day, International Literacy Day, Citizenship Day, Labor Day, and Grandparents Day.

In some schools the values are planned in the following manner:

Beginning of the School Year

All school personnel, students, parents and community are informed of the nine or more core values that will be fostered during the school year. The emphasis is on the "connectedness" of all values. A calendar may be distributed which indicates the values for each month, with special monthly themes, holidays, and topics identified.

Middle of the Year
(January—return from winter break)

School personnel, parents, and students review the values highlighted during the first four months and are reminded of the five values that will be featured in the months of January through June.

End of the School Year
(June)

Some schools devote the last two weeks of school to lessons, activities, and projects connecting all of the values of the year. In addition, some schools send home suggestions and activities so parents will have some help fostering the school/community's core values during the months of July and August.

How can we determine if students have learned and practiced the monthly value? It can be done by observation or by asking parents. However, why not ask students? Having students respond to an evaluation scale similar to the following may provide some useful information. In this scale, the focus is on "responsibility," but it may be used for other values as well.

Evaluating Character Development

Dear Student,

Last month we focused on the value of responsibility. We would appreciate your views about what you learned about responsibility by completing this survey Your name is not necessary. You may wish to make a copy for yourself so you can reflect on your responses as we focus on other values in the months to come.

Directions: The scale has two sets of response items. One asks you to tell us how much you agree or disagree with a statement.

SA = strongly agree   **A = agree**   **N = neutral**
D = disagree   **SD = strongly disagree**

The other response prompt is an incomplete sentence and we ask you to complete the sentence.

Check one: ☐ female   ☐ male   Grade _____

SA   A   N   D   SD   1. I take responsibility for my mistakes.

                        2. Being responsible means _____.

SA   A   N   D   SD   3. I take pride in my schoolwork.

                        4. My classmates seem to view responsibility as _____

                        _____.

SA   A   N   D   SD   5. I come to school with my assignments completed.

                        6. I am a responsible person because _____

                        _____.

SA   A   N   D   SD   7. I am responsible for my behavior in school.

                        8. Activities that have taught me to be responsible are _____

                        _____.

SA   A   N   D   SD   9. I am responsible because I think before I act.

                        10. Responsible people set examples by _____

                        _____.

SA   A   N   D   SD   11. My classmates take responsibility for their actions.

SES 4-8
Student Activities Programs: Questionnaire for Advisors/ Coaches

The research on students who participate in student activities and programs suggests that these students get better grades, are less likely to be truant, and have a stronger attachment to the school. In many instances, student activities, from sports to service clubs, contribute to the social and emotional growth of student-participants.

The central question for the CEEC is: How do the student activities programs (co-curricular) contribute to the school's character education initiatives? Answers to this question must come from advisors, coaches, and students.

There are three ways to seek answers—interviews, surveys, or focus groups. For example, coaches might be brought together as a focus group. In all cases, the guiding questions for the CEEC's use follow. The format below assumes that CEEC will do a survey.

Dear Advisor/Coach,

As you know, the CEEC is responsible for evaluating our school's character education efforts. We need your answers to the following questions to help us determine the extent to which you see your activity/program contributing to students learning and practicing the school's core values. Please answer these questions and return this questionnaire to the secretary or a CEEC member. Thank you for your help in this matter.

_____   _____   _____
(name)   (activity/sport)   (date)

1. How does your activity/sport contribute to our school's character education efforts?

   _____

   _____

   _____

2. How are the core values integrated or highlighted into your activity/program?

   _____

   _____

   _____

3. What do you specifically do to highlight, emphasize, and promote the core values in your program/activity?

   _____

   _____

   _____

4. How would the students in your activity/program respond to questions one and two above?

_____

_____

_____

5. With regard to the school's character education efforts and your activity/program, what are your questions?

_____

_____

_____

_____

What are your concerns?

_____

_____

_____

_____

What are your suggestions?

_____

_____

_____

_____

SES 4-9
Evaluating Curriculum Material

In our *Hearts and Minds* book (see Readings), my co-author and I identified seven standards that we recommended as guidelines for assessing commercial character education programs or materials.

The curriculum/program/materials should:

• foster the school's consensus values.

• be easily integrated with existing state or district standards and frameworks.

• be easy to adapt and revise by teachers at each school site to meet students and program needs.

• include a teacher's guide.

• foster students' critical thinking skills.

• require students to practice the core values.

• be free from bias or prejudice to any individuals or groups. (pp. 75-77)

The evaluation below is an extension of the seven standards and should be used by school stake holders who are expected to use the material on a regular basis. Thus, teachers and students (age appropriate) should be involved in the process. Since parents are expected to play a key role in the school's character education efforts, they too should have an opportunity to review commercial and other curriculum materials before the school adopts them. The scale below is designed for two purposes: 1) to decide whether or not to purchase the material, and/or 2) to determine whether existing material meets the needs of the school's character education efforts. Of course, one of the key questions the CEEC could ask about the commercial material being reviewed is evidence from the publishers that it "works"— however one wants to define that word.

We recommend that this evaluation be completed first by the school's CEEC to determine which items apply to the current or planned program. After review and revision, the evaluation should be given to all teachers, selected students, and members of the school's Parent Teacher Organization for feedback. The results can be used to make decisions regarding materials to purchase.

Evaluating Character Development

Directions: Using the key below, rate the material you are reviewing. Circle the number and write comments. Following each item on the scale, please state your reason for the rating. At the end of the scale, add up your scores and decide whether or not you want to follow the suggestions.

Use this evaluation key:

      0 = Not evident/not for us.

      1 = Needs improving—some of it we can use, some we cannot.

      2 = Good for our purposes with some adaptations

      3 = Excellent—we can use with little or no adaptation.

Respondent:

☐ Teacher   ☐ Student

☐ Parent   ☐ Administrator

Title of the material being reviewed _____

0   1   2   3   1. It supports our school's character education intentions.

                   Reason_____

                   _____

0   1   2   3   2. It supports the core values of our program.

                   Reason_____

                   _____

0   1   2   3   3. It can easily be integrated into our program.

                   Reason_____

                   _____

0   1   2   3   4. It is teacher and student friendly.

                   Reason_____

                   _____

0   1   2   3   5. It provides teachers' guides.

                   Reason_____

                   _____

0   1   2   3   6. It provides testimony from other educators who have used it.

                   Reason_____

                   _____

0   1   2   3   7. The material is well written and graphically pleasing.

                   Reason_____

                   _____

0   1   2   3   8. The language of the material is age appropriate.

                   Reason_____

                   _____

0   1   2   3   9. It can be easily infused/integrated into our program.
                      Reason_____
                      _____

0   1   2   3   10. It has interesting and useful activities for teachers, students, and parents.
                      Reason_____
                      _____

0   1   2   3   11. It will support teachers' attempts to enhance the critical thinking skills of
                      students.
                      Reason_____
                      _____

0   1   2   3   12. It supports some of the existing state or district content standards.
                      Reason_____
                      _____

0   1   2   3   13. It would be a useful add-on to our program.
                      Reason_____
                      _____

0   1   2   3   14. It suggests ways for students to know and do "good."
                      Reason_____
                      _____

Rating Scale Suggestion: Count the number of items rated 3—if you have at least 12, it's a strong recommendation for purchasing the material. If you have more 2s than 3s, make a note of the adaptations that will be necessary and discuss the material. If you have six or more 1s, the material may not be suitable for your school. If you have four or more 0s, return the materials to the publisher.

Section 5 | Instruction

> We worry about what's going into them [students] in the way of curriculum, standards, and incentives, and we worry even more about what comes out, that is, how they score and perform. But we virtually ignore their thoughts and feelings about school.
>
> Eric Schaps, "How Students Experience Their Schools," *Education Week*

Research and best practices tell us that there are instructional strategies that teachers use to enhance the character development of students and to teach the school's core values. These strategies answer the often-asked question, "How do I teach character in my classroom?"

There is so much that can be said about instruction and there is so much that can be evaluated that the best that can be done here is to provide the school's character education evaluation committee with a small sample of possibilities. Many instructional strategies are implied in the items of the instruments that follow.

SES 5-1
Evaluating Curriculum Material

Eric Schaps and his colleagues at the Development Studies Center (Oakland, Calif.) have one of the better researched elementary character education programs in the country. These researchers make a strong case for monitoring and attending to the experiences students have in their schools and classrooms.

The Center's Child Development Project is partially assessed by the use of a two-part questionnaire that evaluates students' perceptions of the extent to which their classmates care about and help one another and the extent to which students' participate in decision making in their class. In essence, the questionnaire evaluates students' sense of community, an important factor in their character development at school.

Respondent:

☐ Teacher/grade _____

☐ Specialist (explain)_____

☐ Other_____

Directions: Read each statement below and circle the number that tells how strongly you agree or disagree with it.

For statements 1 to 14, use this scale:

1 = disagree a lot   2 = disagree a little   3 = don't agree or disagree
4 = agree a little   5 = agree a lot

1	2	3	4	5	1. Students in my class are willing to go out of their way to help someone.
1	2	3	4	5	2. My classmates care about my work just as much as their own.
1	2	3	4	5	3. My class is like a family.
1	2	3	4	5	4. The students in my class don't really care about each other.
1	2	3	4	5	5. A lot of students in my class like to put others down.
1	2	3	4	5	6. Students in my class help each other learn.
1	2	3	4	5	7. Students in my class help each other, even if they are not friends.
1	2	3	4	5	8. Students in my class don't get along together very well.
1	2	3	4	5	9. Students in my class just look out for themselves.
1	2	3	4	5	10. Students in my class are mean to each other.
1	2	3	4	5	11. When I'm having trouble with my work, at least one classmate will try to help.
1	2	3	4	5	12. Students in my class treat each other with respect.
1	2	3	4	5	13. Students in my class work together to solve problems.
1	2	3	4	5	14. When someone in my class does well, everyone in class feels good.

For statements 15 to 24, use this scale:
1= never   2=hardly ever   3 = sometimes
4= often   5 = always

1 2 3 4 5   15. Students have a say in determining what goes on (in my class).

1 2 3 4 5   16. The teacher lets us do things our own way.

1 2 3 4 5   17. The teacher is the only one who decides on the rules.

1 2 3 4 5   18. The teacher lets me choose what I will work on.

1 2 3 4 5   19. The teacher and the students together plan what we will do.

1 2 3 4 5   20. I get to do things that I want to do.

1 2 3 4 5   21. The teacher and the students decide together what the rules will be.

1 2 3 4 5   22. The teacher asks the students to help decide what the class should do.

1 2 3 4 5   23. Students in my class can get a rule changed if they think it is unfair.

1 2 3 4 5   24. Students in my class get to help plan what they will do.

It should be noted by scorers of this instrument that statements 4, 5, 8, 9, 10, 17 are reverse-scored. Also note that the first 14 items address classroom supportiveness and the last 10 items address classroom autonomy and influence.

The questionnaire is reprinted here with permission.

Evaluating Character Development   77

SES 5-2
Teacher Observation Scale

To have rapport with a class is to have the kind of warm, human, and appropriately personal relationship with students that makes it easier for them to talk about problems and be receptive to moral guidance. Without rapport, a teacher's moral influence is greatly diminished.

Tom Lickona, *Educating for Character: How Schools Can Teach Respect and Responsibility*

This observation scale includes items that many researchers say represent behaviors of teachers who attend to the character development of students in their classrooms. A scale of this kind might be used by observers (peers, supervisor, principal) at least four times a year. The observer should discuss ratings with the teacher following each observation.

Observation   September   November   February   April

Teacher _____   Observer_____

Directions: Circle whether you observed the following behaviors in the teacher. Where appropriate, cite an example or incident after each item. If you did not observe the listed behavior in this session, circle NO for Not Observable.

In this observation period, I noticed that this teacher did (D) **or did not** (DN)...

D	DN	NO	1. listen to students.
D	DN	NO	2. motivate students.
D	DN	NO	3. create a sense of caring.
D	DN	NO	4. engage students in purposeful activities.
D	DN	NO	5. employ cooperative learning strategies.
D	DN	NO	6. hold class meetings.
D	DN	NO	7. plan fun activities.
D	DN	NO	8. help students work through behavior problems.
D	DN	NO	9. have students take responsibility for classroom management tasks.
D	DN	NO	10. use student-centered activities.
D	DN	NO	11. create a collaborative classroom climate.
D	DN	NO	12. encourage students to think critically.
D	DN	NO	13. encourage teamwork and sharing among students.
D	DN	NO	14. check for students' understanding of what they are learning.
D	DN	NO	15. check for student understanding of the school's core values.
D	DN	NO	16. reward students for their positive behaviors.
D	DN	NO	17. use effective conflict-resolution strategies.
D	DN	NO	18. show consideration for students' needs.
D	DN	NO	19. ask questions to promote student discussion and reflection.
D	DN	NO	20. encourage students to have dialogue about real-life issues and problems.
D	DN	NO	21. promote in-class service learning activities.
D	DN	NO	22. have clear rules of conduct that students helped create.
D	DN	NO	23. create a classroom where students like to be.
D	DN	NO	24. serve as a model for demonstrating the school's core values.
D	DN	NO	25. establish a language of civility and respectfulness.

SES 5-3
Caring Teacher Inventory

Teachers need to attend to creating a sense of community in the classroom, where mutually respectful relationships are nurtured and prosocial behaviors are welcomed and rewarded.

Edward DeRoche & Mary Williams, *Educating Hearts and Minds*

This self-inventory is based on the research of Kris Bosworth and others who observed 300 classrooms and interviewed more than 100 middle grade students, asking them to identify the characteristics of caring teachers. (See Bosworth, K., in Readings.) The items below are the behaviors the students mentioned. The inventory can be used in staff development or to have students assess their teachers' caring behaviors, but the primary intent is for teachers to use it as a self-evaluation instrument.

Teacher's Grade _____   Subject_____

Directions: Rate the extent to which you use each of these behaviors in your teaching.

1. I help students with their schoolwork.
    ☐ I do this well.   ☐ I don't do enough of this.
    ☐ I really need to work on this.

2. I carefully explain to my students what assignments are about and how to complete them.
    ☐ I do this well.   ☐ I don't do enough of this.
    ☐ I really need to work on this.

3. I continually check to be sure students understand what we are studying and doing.
    ☐ I do this well.   ☐ I don't do enough of this.
    ☐ I really need to work on this.

4. I demonstrate to my students that I value them as individuals.
    ☐ I do this well.   ☐ I don't do enough of this.
    ☐ I really need to work on this.

5. I treat each student with respect.
    ☐ I do this well.   ☐ I don't do enough of this.
    ☐ I really need to work on this.

6. I actively encourage my students to do their best.
    ☐ I do this well.   ☐ I don't do enough of this.
    ☐ I really need to work on this.

7. I take into consideration the amount of homework I give my students.
    ☐ I do this well.   ☐ I don't do enough of this.
    ☐ I really need to work on this.

8. I have no problems giving my students a second chance.
   ☐ I do this well.   ☐ I don't do enough of this.
   ☐ I really need to work on this.

9. I plan some fun activities for the benefit of my students.
   ☐ I do this well.   ☐ I don't do enough of this.
   ☐ I really need to work on this.

10. I really listen to what each student tells me.
    ☐ I do this well.   ☐ I don't do enough of this.
    ☐ I really need to work on this.

11. I help my students set goals and offer advice regarding these goals.
    ☐ I do this well.   ☐ I don't do enough of this.
    ☐ I really need to work on this.

12. I'll go the "extra mile" for my students.
    ☐ I do this well.   ☐ I don't do enough of this.
    ☐ I really need to work on this.

13. I willingly talk to students about their problems.
    ☐ I do this well.   ☐ I don't do enough of this.
    ☐ I really need to work on this.

14. I like being involved with each of my students.
    ☐ I do this well.   ☐ I don't do enough of this.
    ☐ I really need to work on this.

15. I believe in each of my student's capabilities.
    ☐ I do this well.   ☐ I don't do enough of this.
    ☐ I really need to work on this.

16. I like to help each student in any way I can.
    ☐ I do this well.   ☐ I don't do enough of this.
    ☐ I really need to work on this.

Self Rating

After completing this inventory, how would you rate yourself as a caring teacher?
   ☐ Very caring   ☐ Caring
   ☐ Need to work on this   ☐ Not very caring

How would your students rate you as a caring teacher?
   ☐ Among the most caring teachers in this school
   ☐ About average for teacher in this school
   ☐ Something I should work on
   ☐ Not very caring

SES 5-4

Teacher as Model: Students' Views

Dear Student,

This form is a way for me to get feedback about how you see me as a model for demonstrating our school's core values and how you view some of my teaching practices. Circle A (for agree) or D (for disagree) after you read each statement. If you're not sure, circle the letter N.

Your name is not necessary. Thank you for doing this!

Teacher's name _____

A	D	N	1. You really care about each student in this class.
A	D	N	2. You are fair with us.
A	D	N	3. You trust us.
A	D	N	4. You help us make good decisions.
A	D	N	5. You make us think about why we do things.
A	D	N	6. You tell us when we are right or wrong and why.
A	D	N	7. You help us learn to work in groups.
A	D	N	8. You are honest with us.
A	D	N	9. You practice what you preach.
A	D	N	10. You show us how we all can help one another in class.
A	D	N	11. You insist that we use respectful language.
A	D	N	12. You expect all of us to do the best that we can do.
A	D	N	13. You expect us to be respectful and responsible students.
A	D	N	14. When we do the right thing you reward us.
A	D	N	15. You show us how to be proud of our class.

IF YOU CIRCLED D FOR ANY ITEMS, PLEASE EXPLAIN WHY ON THE BACK OF THIS FORM.

Note: Primary grade teachers should use happy face/neutral face/sad face options instead of letters after each item, and reduce the number of items. You may also read the item and have students mark the circle that tells how they feel.

SES 5-5
Teaching Values Reflection Scale

In Section 4, Curriculum and Programs, discussion is centered on the Value-a-Month program and a strategy for evaluating students' self-reflections on the value of responsibility (SES 4-7). In this sample strategy, responsibility is examined from the teaching side using the same format as the students' scale. That is, an opinion statement is followed by an incomplete sentence. This is your reflection instrument. You may share it with others if you wish. Remember the focus here is on the value or trait responsibility. For other values/traits, simply use one of them in place of responsibility.

Directions: Using the response key below, please circle your opinion of each of the following statements.

SA = strongly agree   **A = agree**   **N = no opinion**
D = disagree   **SD = strongly disagree**

SA   A   N   D   SD   1. I model the value of responsibility daily in this school.

2. To me responsibility means _____.

SA   A   N   D   SD   3. There are few on this staff who take this value seriously.

4. Our staff _____.

SA   A   N   D   SD   5. I am pleased with what I teach my students about this value.

6. In this school, responsibility_____.

SA   A   N   D   SD   7. As a result of teaching responsibility, I observe my students being more responsible.

8. My students tell me _____.

SA   A   N   D   SD   9. I have all the materials I needed to teach this value.

10. Responsibility to my students _____.

SA   A   N   D   SD   11. I do not feel adequately prepared to teach this value.

12. To do a better job of teaching responsibility, I need _____.

SA   A   N   D   SD   13. I encourage the parents of students in my class to help me foster this value.

14. In general, the parents' view of holding their child responsible seems to be _____.

SES 5-6
Classroom Climate/ Behaviors: Students' Views

Dear _____,

As you know, during this past year we have made efforts to develop good character and improve relationships in our class. Some of the things that we did were reading stories with moral themes, working on our critical thinking skills, learning how to work cooperatively in groups, holding class meetings, and discussing and practicing the value of the month. Now, I need to know what your views are about our efforts.

Thank you for helping me.

_____(teacher's signature)

Directions: Using the response key below, please circle your opinion of each of the following statements.

SA = strongly agree   A = agree   N = no opinion
D = disagree   SD = strongly disagree

Since the implementation of our class character education efforts, I have seen the following changes in our classroom and my classmates' behavior.

SA	A	N	D	SD	1. There is improvement in my classmates' behavior for the better.
SA	A	N	D	SD	2. My classmates are more willing to help one another.
SA	A	N	D	SD	3. There is better communication between the teacher and the class.
SA	A	N	D	SD	4. There is more participation in class activities.
SA	A	N	D	SD	5. There is less cheating.
SA	A	N	D	SD	6. There is more cooperation among us.
SA	A	N	D	SD	7. We are more willing to resolve our conflicts peacefully.
SA	A	N	D	SD	8. There is greater participation in group projects.
SA	A	N	D	SD	9. There are fewer classroom disruptions.
SA	A	N	D	SD	10. There is greater use of civil, respectful language.
SA	A	N	D	SD	11. There are fewer put-downs and harassment.
SA	A	N	D	SD	12. We are all more respectful.
SA	A	N	D	SD	13. There is greater appreciation of the traits of good character.
SA	A	N	D	SD	14. We are better at thinking before acting.
SA	A	N	D	SD	15. There is more collaborative planning with our teacher.
SA	A	N	D	SD	16. We have a much better attitude toward learning.
SA	A	N	D	SD	17. There is a sense that we are responsible for one another.
SA	A	N	D	SD	18. We pay attention more than we did.
SA	A	N	D	SD	19. More students complete their assignments.
SA	A	N	D	SD	20. There is more sharing of our concerns/problems.

SES 5-7
Observation Checklist: Students Practicing Values

This checklist is one way for you to record your observations of your students demonstrating the value being studied in a particular month. There are four weeks in the month, so you have four opportunities to record your observations. So, rather than carrying this instrument with you each day (unless you want to be more precise), it is recommended that each week you take about 15 minutes and think about your students and their behaviors and actions that relate to the value that month. For example, let us say that the value of the month value is responsibility. List on the form below the students you have observed demonstrating responsibility, and where you saw it occur.

I have observed this student demonstrating the value of responsibility:

      A = in the classroom
      B = in the corridor
      C = on the playground
      D = in the cafeteria
      E = at assemblies
      F = in group work
      G = in co-curricular activities
      H = doing school projects
      I = doing classroom projects
      J = other_____(specify)

Place letter(s) on line below week of observation.

STUDENT'S NAME	WEEK	1	2	3	4
_____		____	____	____	____
_____		____	____	____	____
_____		____	____	____	____
_____		____	____	____	____
_____		____	____	____	____
_____		____	____	____	____

Reflection questions:

- What does the information above tell you?
- What do you plan to do with the information?
- Do you think you should share it with individual students?
- Do you plan to share it with the class without mentioning specific student names?
- How would you modify this instrument to better meet your needs for observing students demonstrating the school's core values?

SES 5-8
Student Self-Assessment: Working in Groups

Dear _____,

    As you know, I often use cooperative learning groups. I like the idea of group work for many reasons, but I need to know how you see yourself in these groups. Please fill out the form below and return it to me. Thank you.

_____(teacher's signature)

Directions: Put a check mark on one of the four words that tells how you feel.

1. I ☐ always ☐ usually ☐ sometimes ☐ never like working in cooperative learning groups.

2. I ☐ always ☐ usually ☐ sometimes ☐ never try to keep my group on task.

3. I ☐ always ☐ usually ☐ sometimes ☐ never take a leadership role.

4. I ☐ always ☐ usually ☐ sometimes ☐ never make useful suggestions.

5. I ☐ always ☐ usually ☐ sometimes ☐ never encourage others to work together.

6. I ☐ always ☐ usually ☐ sometimes ☐ never work with my group to finish a project on time.

7. I ☐ always ☐ usually ☐ sometimes ☐ never respect the opinions of members of my group.

8. I ☐ always ☐ usually ☐ sometimes ☐ never will do extra work for the group's benefit.

9. If I were to grade my group for its work, I would give it an   A B C D F (circle one).

10. For the work I have done in my group, I would give myself a grade of
_____.

Optional: In my group these students have earned a grade of

A _____

B _____

C _____

D or F _____

SES 5-9
Instructional Strategies Checklist

To the Teacher: This checklist offers instructional ideas and calls for you to reflect on ways that you teach the school's core values. Your task is to check those activities under each of the seven strategies that you now employ. Consider those strategies that you didn't check as possibilities. Then, in the space provided, or on the back of this form, add others that came to mind after reading the list of activities. Below are some ways that answer the question: How do I teach character/values to my students?

To CEEC: If teachers are willing to share their lists (names not necessary), the committee could create a list of classroom strategies that have been used and suggested by the teachers at the school. Then teachers will have a good idea of what others are doing and all teachers will have a repertoire of activities to draw upon to support their efforts teaching the school's core values.

Here's what I do to teach the school's core values:

1. By having moral conversations that include
   - ☐ personal and family stories
   - ☐ telling and listening
   - ☐ holding dilemma discussions
   - ☐ discussing what's right/wrong; legal/ethical, good/bad; just/unjust
   - ☐ using teachable moments
   - ☐ reflecting on what motivates people
   - ☐ reflecting on student behaviors

   I would add these activities _____

   _____

   _____

2. By modeling
   - ☐ practicing, not preaching
   - ☐ showing students how the values guide your actions
   - ☐ helping students see how others (literature, history, or real life) demonstrate the values

   I would add these activities _____

   _____

   _____

3. By interactions/relationships
   - ☐ showing positive or negative reactions to student behaviors
   - ☐ correcting poor behavior
   - ☐ praising positive behavior
   - ☐ using appropriate rewards and punishments
   - ☐ helping students see the relationship between choice and consequences
   - ☐ promoting positive social interactions in classroom
   - ☐ holding class meetings

   I would add these activities _____

   _____

   _____

4. By reading
   ☐ using a literature-based curriculum
   ☐ using film and video that provide moral lessons
   ☐ using newspaper and magazines

   I would add these activities _____
   _____
   _____

5. By writing
   ☐ journal-writing to help students hone thinking skills
   ☐ to help students focus on feelings/actions of characters in literature
   ☐ to help students think about their choices and decisions
   ☐ to develop students' moral reasoning skills
   ☐ personal journals to help students reflect on who they are and what they want to become

   I would add these activities _____
   _____
   _____

6. By participation
   ☐ in classroom management activities
   ☐ in cooperative learning projects
   ☐ in completing assignments
   ☐ in helping classmates
   ☐ in student-initiated community projects

   I would add these activities _____
   _____
   _____

7. By special activities
   ☐ special projects based on themes of the calendar (e.g., Black History Month
   ☐ classroom meetings
   ☐ guest speakers
   ☐ parental involvement
   ☐ time management instruction
   ☐ conflict resolution
   ☐ anger management
   ☐ drug use and abuse instruction
   ☐ social skills development

   I would add these activities _____
   _____
   _____

Section 6 | Partnerships

A starting point for any effort to improve the character of our youth is the realization that good character is not inherited; it must be taught. In the home, in the classroom, in religious institutions, and in the community, adults must deliberately and diligently teach what it means to a be a person of good character.

Helen LeGette, *Parents, Kids, and Character:*
21 Strategies to Help Your Children Develop Good Character

One character education axiom is that effective programs have strong and meaningful partnerships with parents and the community. In reality, character education is a community affair. While the home and school take the lead in fostering good character among the young, it is the community (neighborhood, media, malls, marketplace, peer groups, gangs) that also influences young people's values. Some say community influence in shaping values is stronger than both the home and school.

The community needs to know what the school is doing to promote good character. A community that has resources and services can help families and schools. Businesses, agencies, faith communities, and others must be encouraged to form partnerships addressing the physical and social/emotional health of their community's youth. Service learning, for example, has become a vehicle for strengthening school-community partnerships.

Schools with character education initiatives have recognized the importance of involving parents and the community. A litany of partnership activities can be found in most books on character education, as well in lists of best practices. Not generally available to stake holders who engage in parental and community character-building activities are ways to evaluate their partnership efforts.

Seek out partnerships with businesses and higher education institutions that can provide assessment advice and assistance. In colleges and universities, there are professors who do research and evaluation for a living.

Many businesses have research and development departments with an array of talent that can be tapped by the school's evaluation committee. These are the evaluation partnerships that the school's character education committee will find valuable and should seek out.

In order to help you and the character education evaluation committee assess character education partnership efforts, particularly with parents, six evaluation strategy examples follow.

SES 6-1
Community Partnership Overview

Here is a series of suggestions and questions that the character education evaluation committee should use as a first step in assessing community partnership activities at the school.

1. What groups/organizations are involved in partnership activities with the school? (This will be List 1.)

2. From the list above, note those groups and organizations that are directly connected to the school's character education initiatives. (This will be List 2.)

3. For each of the groups/organizations on List 2, describe the specific activities it provides in support of the school's character education efforts.

4. In the opinion of CEEC's members, which group/organization(s) appears to be most effective? (Make a judgment with or without hard evidence.)

5. Which appear to be least effective?

6. How would the committee members rate the communication between school personnel and partnership personnel regarding the school's character education efforts?

7. How do parents, teachers, and students view the school's character education partnerships? Answer this question by examining data from the instruments below.

8. Given the committee members' views on effectiveness and communication, what are the next steps the committee should take to strengthen, maintain, or cease the partnership with a specific group or organization?

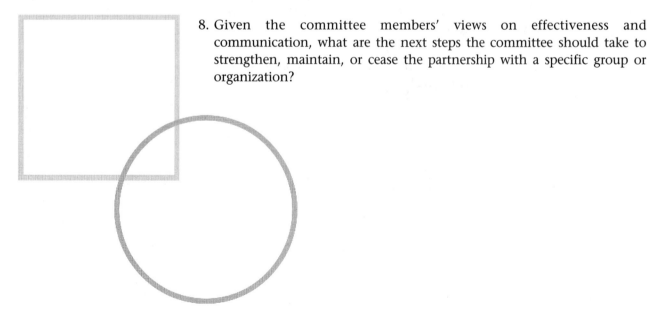

SES 6-2
Partner's Interview Questionnaire

Each year, the CEEC should ensure that groups and organizations in partnership with the school in its work in character education have an opportunity to share their opinions about the relationship. There are several ways to do this. One common way is to have one or two members of the CEEC interview personnel from an organization or community group about the relationship. The interview should take about an hour. The interview questions should be common for all groups/organizations so comparisons may be made, if necessary.

1. Knowledge: Tell us what you know about our school's character education efforts.

2. Activities: What has your group/organization been doing to support our character education efforts?

3. Contacts: Whom do you contact at the school with regard to the partnership?

4. Communication: How would you rate our communication with your group/organization? How would you rate your communication with us?

5. Satisfaction: Are you satisfied with the partnership arrangements? If yes, why? If not, why not?

6. Assistance: What can we do to maintain or strengthen the partnership? Have we responded adequately to your requests throughout the year? What information do you need in order to enhance your service to the school?

7. Is there anything else you wish to share with us about our partnership with you?

SES 6-3
The 3 I's

Only three words are necessary to engage parents in the school's efforts to educate its students regarding character. They are: *Invite, Inform,* and *Involve*! In this instrument, we try to determine the opinions of the respondents regarding the practices implied by these three words.

Respondent:
☐ Parent   ☐ Teacher
☐ Administrator   ☐ Other (specify) _____

Directions: Please circle the letter(s) that tells the extent of agreement with the statement.

SA = strongly agree   **A= agree**   **N= neutral**
D= disagree   **SD= strongly disagree**

This school's character education effort has...

SA   A   N   D   SD   1. increased parent attendance at parent-teacher conferences.

Comment: _____

_____

SA   A   N   D   SD   2. increased parent attendance at most school events.

Comment: _____

_____

SA   A   N   D   SD   3. strengthened the relationship between teachers and parents.

Comment: _____

_____

SA   A   N   D   SD   4. helped parents become more involved in their child's school activities/work.

Comment: _____

_____

SA   A   N   D   SD   5. enhanced parental awareness about their child's behaviors.

Comment: _____

_____

SA   A   N   D   SD   6. brought forth many positive comments about the program.

Comment: _____

_____

SA   A   N   D   SD   7. encouraged parents to talk about values/virtues with their child.

Comment: _____

_____

SA   A   N   D   SD   8. inspired parents to help their children practice the core values/traits at home.

Comment: _____

_____

SA   A   N   D   SD   9. strong support from all parents.

Comment: _____

_____

Are there any further comments you would like to share about parental involvement and support of our school's character education efforts?

_____

_____

_____

_____

_____

SES 6-4
Parents' Perceptions

Dear Parent/Guardian:

The Character Education Committee seeks your opinions regarding this school's character education efforts. As you know, the school and community have identified these virtues to be the focus of the program: [Committee note: List virtues here—in some schools they are called traits, in others they are called values.] Since the program began, we have sought your participation and support. Once again we call on you to help us. This questionnaire will provide important information that we need from you and other parents to help us in our continuing efforts to make the program better. Please take a few minutes to fill out this questionnaire, place it in the envelope, and have your child give it to the school secretary or his/her classroom teacher. Your name is not necessary. Thank you for helping us.

Directions: Tell us the extent to which you agree or disagree with the following statements.

SA = strongly agree   **A= agree**   **N= neutral**
D= disagree   **SD= strongly disagree**

SA A N D SD   1. My child and I seem to have more conversations about right and wrong behavior.

SA A N D SD   2. My child and I have had more discussions about virtues such as respect and responsibility.

SA A N D SD   3. Since the character education program was implemented, this school seems to be a safer and more pleasant place for my child and me.

SA A N D SD   4. My child seems to be in better control of his/her emotions because of the character education program.

SA A N D SD   5. I really believe that the focus on the teaching and learning of the core virtues in the school and in my child's classroom is contributing to his/her academic success.

SA A N D SD   6. My child's teacher and I have been working together to teach the core virtues of the program.

SA A N D SD   7. The school's parent programs about character development and character education have really been helpful to my family.

SA A N D SD   8. I haven't really found enough time to get involved in this program.

SA A N D SD   9. I want to get involved in the character education of my child but school personnel have not made an effort to help me do so.

SA A N D SD   10. It seems to me that the school should focus on academic development and leave character development to parents and others.

Here are my recommendations to make the character education program better than it is right now:_____

_____

_____

_____

Evaluating Character Development   95

SES 6-5
Parents' Survey: Elementary School

Carla Berk, a teacher and member of Ivey Ranch Elementary (California) School's Character Education Committee, conducted a survey of 600 parents regarding the school's climate. The survey and comments are printed with her permission. While our focus here is the instrument, her commentary about findings are of equal interest.

Ms. Berk says that the results of the survey were not surprising. The parents were very supportive of the school's efforts to be a caring, safe, and enriching environment. She noted that both the Character Education Committee and the teachers were pleased with the level of parent support on most of the survey items. The results, she says, were encouraging to teachers and made them want to continue their efforts. The survey showed two areas that need attention. One was the peer relationships between older and younger students and thus the need to consider a school-wide "peer-buddies" program. A second was the need for more resources from parents.

Dear Parents,

The Character Education Committee is very interested in your viewpoint regarding our school's climate. Based on your own observations, tell us whether you agree or disagree with the following statements about our school. Please give your honest opinion. Thank you for your help.

Directions: Tell us the extent to which you agree or disagree with the following statements.

1 = strongly agree	2 = agree	3 = neutral
4 = disagree	5 = strongly disagree	DK = don't know

1   2   3   4   5   DK   1. Caring relationships between adults and students are important at our school.

1   2   3   4   5   DK   2. Caring and positive relationships between students are important at our school.

1   2   3   4   5   DK   3. Our school makes it a high priority to help form positive relationships between older and younger students.

1   2   3   4   5   DK   4. Our school does not tolerate disrespect and takes steps to prevent and deal with it effectively when it occurs.

1   2   3   4   5   DK   5. Students are provided with many opportunities for character development, such as cooperative learning, conflict resolution, class problem-solving meetings, classroom helper jobs, peer tutoring, and school and community service.

1   2   3   4   5   DK   6. Our academic curriculum is designed to challenge all students to do their personal best and develop the qualities of character.

1   2   3   4   5   DK   7. Our school's approach to classroom and school discipline is centered on developing student commitment to doing what is right.

1   2   3   4   5   DK   8. Logical consequences for wrongdoing are handled respectfully.

1 2 3 4 5 DK   9. Students are involved in leadership roles (e.g., through student council, community service, peer-mediation, and extracurricular activities) in ways that develop their responsibility.

1 2 3 4 5 DK   10. The staff has a positive attitude when dealing with each other, students, parents, and the community.

1 2 3 4 5 DK   11. Our school offers parents support such as books, tapes, counseling, community services and other resources that help parents develop skills and strengthen their relationship with their child.

1 2 3 4 5 DK   12. Our students benefit from family activities at this school.

Comments:

_____

_____

_____

SES 6-6

Teacher/ Student Perceptions of Partnerships

Respondent:

☐ Teacher   ☐ Student, grade: _____

Dear Teacher or Student:

Below is a list of partnerships that are designed to help support the school's character education efforts. [List school's partnerships here] Please evaluate our partnerships by completing the items that follow. Thank you for your help.

1. Which partnerships do you feel are essential to our character education efforts?

2. Which partnerships probably do not contribute much to the school's character education efforts?

3. What do students (classmates) say about participation in some of the activities with the school's partners?

4. What do teachers say about the partnerships?

5. Which partnerships do you suggest be continued? Which partnerships would you drop or change?

6. What are your suggestions for improving the partnerships list above?

7. What new community partnerships do you think the school should seek out?

SES 6-7
Parents' Survey: Dearborn Public Schools

In 1991, the superintendent of the Dearborn (Michigan) Public Schools formed a character education committee of educators and parents and, after surveying the community, five values were selected to be infused into school activities. The following survey instrument is sent to parents every other year.

Dear Parent:

Character Education is an important part of the Dearborn Public Schools. The program emphasizes five core values. These values—honesty, integrity, respect for self and others, responsibility, and courtesy—are at the heart of this program. These five core values are taught throughout the entire curriculum instead of teaching Character Education as a separate subject. Please take a few minutes to complete this survey and send it back to school. This survey is designed to be an assessment of parental opinion regarding Dearborn's Character Education Program.

Directions: For each question, please circle Yes, No or Not Sure.

Yes   No   Not Sure   1. Have you seen the posters identifying the five core values in the schools?

Yes   No   Not Sure   2. Do you believe character education will have a positive influence on your child?

Yes   No   Not Sure   3. Do you think the public schools should be concerned about teaching values to children in school?

Yes   No   Not Sure   4. Do you think incorporating these five core values has a positive influence on your child?

Yes   No   Not Sure   5. Do you think we need to be pro-active toward improving moral values in our society?

Yes   No   Not Sure   6. Do you think student behavior has improved since the implementation of our Character Education Program?

Yes   No   Not Sure   7. Are you aware the Dearborn Public Schools has distributed to every family the Code of Conduct manual outlining expectations for behavior and consequences for the violation of rules?

Yes   No   Not Sure   8. Does your child understand the rules of behavior that exist in our school?

Yes   No   Not Sure   9. Are there consistent consequences for misbehavior?

Yes   No   Not Sure   10. Do you think your child is developing a sensitivity to the needs and feelings of others?

Yes   No   Not Sure   11. Does your child talk about the character education activities happening in our school? (plays, assemblies, art and literacy projects, collections for the needy, etc.)

Yes   No   Not Sure   12. Do you feel your children are in a school environment where they have the opportunity to resolve conflicts and problems with adult support?

Yes   No   Not Sure   13. Is your child becoming more skilled at solving problems on his/her own?

Please share any comments and/or questions on the back of this questionnaire.

Section 7	# Evaluation

In this last section of the book, which I hope you find to be a useful guide on your evaluation journey, the focus will be on evaluation principles and practices. The Character Education Partnership (CEP) offers eleven principles of character education. Three character education experts—Thomas Lickona, Eric Schaps, and Cathy Lewis—wrote the CEP guide. These experts suggest that the eleven principles are essential to any school or district's character education initiatives. Therefore, a school's Character Education Evaluation Committee should review, or rather study, these guidelines carefully and use them as evaluative methods of determining program effectiveness.

This section, then, has three suggested evaluation strategies that use one or all of CEP eleven principles. These three strategies are followed by two instruments—one used by a school district, another used by a middle school. This section ends with an "organizer" that the school's Character Education Evaluation Committee should use to assess its current and future evaluation plans.

SES 7-1
Guiding Principles for Evaluation

CEP's Principle 11 addresses the importance of evaluation processes and results. It is reprinted here in its entirety with permission from CEP.

PRINCIPLE 11

Evaluation of character education should assess the character of the school, the school staff's functioning as character educators, and the extent to which students manifest good character. Effective character education must include an effort to assess progress. Three broad kinds of outcomes merit attention:

The character of the school:

To what extent is the school becoming a more caring community? This can be assessed, for example, with surveys that ask students to indicate the extent to which they agree with statement such as, "Students in this school (classroom) respect and care about each other," and "This school (classroom) is like a family."

The school staff's growth as character educators:

To what extent have adult staff—teaching faculty, administrators, and support personnel—developed understandings of what they can do to foster character development? Personal commitment to do so? Skills to carry it out? Consistent habits of acting upon their developing capacities as character educators?

Student character:

To what extent do students manifest understanding of, commitment to, and action upon the core ethical values? Schools can, for example, gather data on various character-related behaviors. Has student attendance gone up? Have fights and suspensions gone down? Has vandalism declined? Have drug incidents diminished?

Schools can assess the three domains of character (knowing, feeling, and behaving) through anonymous questionnaires that measure student moral judgment (for example, "Is cheating on a test wrong?"), moral commitment (Would you cheat if you were sure you wouldn't get caught?) and self-reported moral behavior (How many times have you cheated on a test or major assignment in the past year?). Such questionnaires can be administered at the beginning of a school's character initiative to get a baseline and again at later points to assess progress.

SES 7-2
Guiding Questions for Character Education Initiatives

Other Character Education Partnership principles for judging the effectiveness of your school's character education efforts are stated below in question form for evaluative use by the committee. (They are reprinted with permission.)

1. Do the character education efforts promote core ethical values as the basis of good character?

2. Is it clear to stake holders that the core values transcend religious and cultural traditions and principles?

3. Has the school identified, defined, and publicly promoted the core values?

4. Are all school members held accountable for upholding conduct consistent with the school's core values?

5. Do the character education initiatives encompass the cognitive, emotional, and behavioral aspects of good character?

6. Do school members take an intentional proactive and comprehensive approach?
   a. Are there plans that show deliberate ways to develop students' character?
   b. Are the core values integrated in every aspect of school life?
   c. Is there a comprehensive, holistic approach to the school's character education programs and activities?

7. Is the school a caring, civil, and just community?
   a. Is there evidence of caring relationships among teachers, students, parents, and others?
   b. Are the core values imbedded in the daily life of the school?

8. Do students have opportunities to apply the core values they are learning?

9. Is cooperative learning a part of the instructional process?

10. Are there service learning projects where students can apply the core values learned?

11. Do students have opportunities to learn and practice prosocial skills? Emotional control? Anger management?

12. Is there a strong, positive connection between the academic curriculum and character education?

13. Do teachers see character education as an integral part of a meaningful and challenging curriculum, or do teachers view it as an add-on?
   a. Are the character education initiatives integrated in the teaching-learning processes?
   b. Does the academic curriculum embody the core values of the character education program?

14. Do the character education initiatives foster students' intrinsic motivation?

Evaluating Character Development   103

15. Are extrinsic rewards and punishments minimized?

16. Do the discipline approaches promote a commitment to the core values?

17. Do rule-breaking procedures contribute to students' understandings and responsibilities?

18. Do all of the adults at the school take ownership of the character education efforts?

    a. Do relationships among the staff embody the school's core values?

    b. Does the staff have time and resources to reflect on their role as models for and mentors of students?

19. Are there leaders at the school who champion efforts to develop the character of students?

    a. Are students given opportunities to assume leadership roles?

20. Are parents and the community invited to be active participants in the school's character-building efforts?

    a. Are parent representatives on the character education committee?

21. Are businesses, religious institutions, youth organizations, governmental agencies, and the media recruited to promote the school's core values and its character education efforts?

22. Does the school have an evaluation plan to assess progress?

SES 7-3

Evaluating Principles Scale

Thomas Lickona designed an evaluation instrument based on Character Education Partnership's eleven principles. He recommends using it as a self-assessment instrument or one that may be used by an outside observer. I have summarized only the sub-components of this evaluation principle to give you a sense of the usefulness of the instrument for evaluating your school's character education efforts. The summary of Principle 11 on evaluation is reprinted with permission from Professor Lickona.

To obtain the "Eleven Principles Survey" at no cost, contact the Center for the 4th & 5th Rs, SUNY Cortland, P.O. Box 2000, Cortland, NY 13045, 607-753-2455.

Respondent:

☐ CEEC member   ☐ Teacher
☐ Administrator   ☐ Counselor

Directions: Please complete this scale below and return it to the CEEC or the school secretary.

The rating scale for each principle and its sub-components is:

1= low implementation   **3= moderate implementation**
5 = high implementation   **DK = don't know**

1   2   3   4   5   DK   1. Our program assesses the character of our school as a moral community.

1   2   3   4   5   DK   2. Our staff periodically engages in systematic assessment of our program... (and uses) the results of these assessments...to plan program improvements.

1   2   3   4   5   DK   3. Our school asks staff to report...their efforts periodically to implement character education.

1   2   3   4   5   DK   4. We assess our students' progress in developing an understanding of the character traits.

1   2   3   4   5   DK   5. We assess our students' progress in developing an emotional attachment and commitment to the qualities of good character....

1   2   3   4   5   DK   6. We assess our students' progress in behaving in ways that reflect the character traits.

1   2   3   4   5   DK   7. We include assessment of student character as part of our report card.

SES 7-4
Self-Assessment Instrument: Lawrence Township

The self-assessment instrument that follows is a modification (for a school site) of an instrument used by the Lawrence Township School District (Indiana) for its award-winning character education efforts. Duane E. Hodgin, Ph.D., the district's assistant superintendent and noted speaker on character education, granted permission to modify the instrument for this book.

Directions for using the instrument asked respondents to determine the extent to which each of the 11 principles for program effectiveness (see CEP) have been implemented by providing some evidence of the implementation, and then to rate the degree to which the implementation has been effective.

For a school site, the CEEC might ask teachers, for example, to respond to the instrument that follows. (Note one major advantage of the instrument—the need for the respondent to provide evidence of principle implementation in addition to assess implementation effectiveness.)

Scale: 5 = Exceptional implementation
4 = Very good implementation
3 = Good implementation
2 = Fair implementation
1 = Poor implementation (little evidence that this principle was implemented)

Our school's character education initiative...

5 4 3 2 1   1. Promotes core ethical values as the basis of good character.
The evidence that we implemented this principle includes:

_____
_____
_____

5 4 3 2 1   2. Is comprehensively defined to include the actions of "thinking," "feeling," and "behaving."
The evidence that we implemented this principle includes:

_____
_____
_____

5 4 3 2 1   3. Requires an intentional, proactive, and comprehensive approach that promotes the core values in all phases of school life.
The evidence that we implemented this principle includes:

_____
_____
_____

5   4   3   2   1   4. Fosters and promotes the school as a caring community.
The evidence that we implemented this principle includes:

_____

_____

_____

5   4   3   2   1   5. Provides students with opportunities for moral action.
The evidence that we implemented this principle includes:

_____

_____

_____

5   4   3   2   1   6. Includes a meaningful and challenging academic curriculum that
respects all learners and helps them to succeed.
The evidence that we implemented this principle includes:

_____

_____

_____

5   4   3   2   1   7. Strives to develop students' intrinsic (internal) motivation.
The evidence that we implemented this principle includes:

_____

_____

_____

5   4   3   2   1   8. Has led to a learning and moral community in which all share
responsibility for character education and all attempt to adhere to the
same core values that guide the education of students.
The evidence that we implemented this principle includes:

_____

_____

_____

5   4   3   2   1   9. Requires moral leadership from school personnel and parents.
The evidence that we implemented this principle includes:

_____

_____

_____

5 4 3 2 1   10. Recruits parents and community members as full partners in the character-building effort.
The evidence that we implemented this principle includes:

_____

_____

_____

5 4 3 2 1   11. Recognizes the importance of evaluating and assessing the character of the school, the school staff's functioning as character educators, and the extent to which students manifest good character.
The evidence that we implemented this principle includes:

_____

_____

_____

SES 7-5
The Greenfield Way: A Character Education Program Evaluation

(Teachers' Perceptions)

Jenny Ferrone, a doctoral candidate at the University of San Diego and a mechanical engineer, conducted a study of the Greenfield Middle School's (El Cajon, Calif.) character education program. The purpose of the study was to determine teacher perceptions of the school's character education program called "The Greenfield Way (TGW). The school's character education efforts are designed to enable students to

1. interact effectively and successfully with others.
2. feel connected to school.
3. learn specific behaviors that demonstrate the character traits defined in The Greenfield Way.
4. develop positive feelings toward themselves, their school, and their community.

The Greenfield Way is a values-based program focusing on a value-of-the-month. The values/traits included in the program are: courtesy, commitment, respect, appreciation, initiative, responsibility, honesty, self-discipline, cooperation and success. The Greenfield Way is taught through a variety of student activities targeting student behaviors as key goals. Activities include role plays, discussion, readings, writings, skits, debates, research projects, daily logs, art projects and guest speakers to name a few. School-wide reinforcement procedures support, encourage, and recognize outstanding student behavior. The P.A. system, rather than paper bulletins, offers a daily "Thought for the Day" and reading selections in support of the Value of the Month.

The school principal was interested in teachers' perceptions of TGW and Ms. Ferrone was interested in doing a research project on character education. As a result, Ms. Ferrone met with the principal and designed a study plan and an assessment instrument that was based on interviews, document reading, and a site visit. After several sessions with the principal, permission was granted to survey the teachers with the instrument shown below. It is reprinted here with their permission.

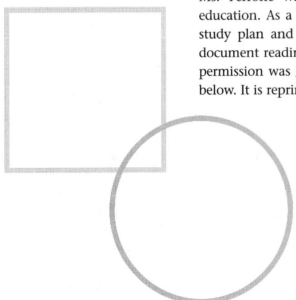

Evaluating Character Development

THE GREENFIELD WAY

Program Effectiveness

Dear Teacher,

As you know, our character education program, The Greenfield Way (TGW), has been part of this school's efforts for the past two years. It is time to do an "audit"—to get your opinions about the program and our effort to influence the behaviors of our students.

It is important to all of us that you take a few minutes to complete this survey carefully and completely. We will collate the information received from you and other teachers and provide you with a report on where we are perceived to be and what we need to do to improve/enhance our efforts to foster the character development of Greenfield students.

Please return to_____ by _____

Teacher name (optional): _____

Years at Greenfield School (check one)

☐ 5 or less years   ☐ more than 5 years

Directions: Please indicate how you feel about each of the following statements. Circle one for each item.

SA = strongly agree   A = agree   D = disagree

SD = strongly disagree   DN = don't know or no opinion

About Students

1. Since TGW was implemented, the students in our school show more:

courtesy	SA	A	D	SD	DN
commitment	SA	A	D	SD	DN
respect	SA	A	D	SD	DN
appreciation	SA	A	D	SD	DN
initiative	SA	A	D	SD	DN
responsibility	SA	A	D	SD	DN
self-discipline	SA	A	D	SD	DN
honesty	SA	A	D	SD	DN
cooperation	SA	A	D	SD	DN
success	SA	A	D	SD	DN

2. Since TGW was implemented, the students in our school show improvement in their:

academic achievement	SA	A	D	SD	DN
motivation for school work	SA	A	D	SD	DN
cooperative learning activities	SA	A	D	SD	DN
relationships among students	SA	A	D	SD	DN
critical thinking skills	SA	A	D	SD	DN
understanding of core values	SA	A	D	SD	DN
respect for school property	SA	A	D	SD	DN

Goals   **Directions:** Please assess the extent to which you think we are working towards the goals of TGW.

1. ☐ Most ☐ some ☐ few ☐ none of the students are interacting effectively with one another.

2. ☐ Most ☐ some ☐ few ☐ none of the students feel connected to this school.

3. ☐ Most ☐ some ☐ few ☐ none of the students have developed positive feeling about themselves.

4. ☐ Most ☐ some ☐ few ☐ none of the students have improved their relationships with one another.

5. ☐ Most ☐ some ☐ few ☐ none of the students have developed positive feelings about the Greenfield community.

6. ☐ Most ☐ some ☐ few ☐ none of the students are learning and practicing the monthly values of TGW program.

Implementation   **Directions:** Please tell us to what extent TGW program meets each of the following statements. Circle one number per item.
5 = To a great extent   3 = To some extent   1 = Hardly ever

5	4	3	2	1	1. The program is well organized.
5	4	3	2	1	2. Teachers are committed to TGW.
5	4	3	2	1	3. The administration provides leadership for the program.
5	4	3	2	1	4. Students are actively involved.
5	4	3	2	1	5. TGW is meeting its goals.
5	4	3	2	1	6. Teachers support all ten values (traits) of the program.
5	4	3	2	1	7. Teachers integrate the values into the daily activities of their classrooms.
5	4	3	2	1	8. Teachers infuse the curriculum with the values highlighted each month.
5	4	3	2	1	9. Each team has planned activities for the value of the month.
5	4	3	2	1	10. Parents support TGW.
5	4	3	2	1	11. Teachers use "teachable moments" to teach a particular value.
5	4	3	2	1	12. To what extent has TGW been integrated into the curriculum and daily activities of the school.
5	4	3	2	1	13. Each team plans to integrate the trait of the month into their classroom activities.
5	4	3	2	1	14. Each team tries to integrate the trait of the month into the curriculum.

Evaluating Character Development   **111**

5 4 3 2 1   15. Each team determines recognition activities for rewarding students who demonstrates the monthly trait.

5 4 3 2 1   16. Teachers use the TGW handbook to select and use activities for the trait of the month.

5 4 3 2 1   17. Teachers use a variety of ways to help students learn and practice the trait of the month.

5 4 3 2 1   18. Each week team members nominate a student to be the "Thunderbirds of the Month."

5 4 3 2 1   19. Each month, each team implements a recognition/reward activity for selected students.

Questions

Directions: Please provide a brief statement or Yes/No to the following questions.

1. What are the benefits of TGW?

_____

_____

2. Is TGW changing the behaviors of the students?_____

3. What is needed to improve TGW?

_____

_____

4. Are the goals and expectation of TGW clear to students? ☐ Yes ☐ No

to parents? ☐ Yes ☐ No

to teachers? ☐ Yes ☐ No

5. Is there total support to TGW by teachers? ☐ Yes ☐ Somewhat ☐ No
If no, why not? _____

_____

Goals

Directions: Which TGW goals do you feel needs greater attention by teachers and the administration? Select 2 with check marks.

☐ students' relationships with one another

☐ students' connections to the school

☐ values of the month idea

☐ students' self-esteem

☐ students' attitudes about the school

☐ students' feeling about the community

Your Opinion

1. In your opinion, what benefits have you seen?

_____

_____

_____

_____

_____

_____

2. What are the program's strengths?

_____

_____

_____

_____

_____

_____

3. What are the program's weaknesses?

_____

_____

_____

_____

_____

_____

4. Where would you like to see improvement?

_____

_____

_____

_____

_____

_____

SES 7-6
Year-End Evaluation Organizer

The Character Education Evaluation Committee has finished its year's work. It is now time for the committee to meet and review what has been accomplished and what remains to be done. This organizer may help the committee focus its review efforts.

Step 1: Review ES 1—Framework

Step 2: Review ES 2—Organizing questions

Step 3: Review ES 3—Guiding principles for evaluation

Step 4: Review ES 4—Evaluating questions

Step 5: Review ES 5—Evaluating principles

Step 6: Use the following organizing questions to close out the year and then go enjoy the summer.

- What components of the program did we evaluate this year?

- What did we find out from this evaluation work?

- How did we use the information/findings?

- How effective was our communication of the findings with our stake holders?

- What changes could or should we have made as we conducted our evaluation?

- What now needs to be changed or improved?

- What are our suggestions for next year's evaluation efforts?

- How shall we prepare now for next year's evaluation plans?

For the School's Character Education Evaluation Library

The school's character education evaluation committee should create a resource library for use by all stake holders involved in the evaluation efforts at the school. The list below provides a mere sampling of the many character education resources that should be part of the evaluation library. The list annotates one or two examples from organizations, businesses, individuals, and schools districts to illustrate the variety of instruments available.

ADDITIONAL INSTRUMENTS

Anderson, L. & Bourke, S. (2000). *Assessing Affective Characteristics in the Schools*. Rahway, N.J.: Lawrence Erbaum Associates. The authors provide a 39-item instrument called "The Quality of School Life" for students. The instrument provides information on seven scales: general, negative affect, teachers, social integration, and opportunity.

Bulach, C. *A Survey of Behavioral Characteristics of Students*. State University of West Georgia. The survey instrument assesses students' attitudes and behaviors, and 17 traits/values such as honesty, responsibility, and integrity. Professor Bulach has also developed the following data-collection instruments: "Instructional Improvement Survey," "Group Openness and Trust," "Leadership Behavior," "Caring Behaviors," "Character Traits," and "Bullying Behaviors." www.westga/~cbulach/

Character Education Partnership. In addition to the booklet and toolkit referred to elsewhere in this book, CEP provides a self-assessment tool for schools and school districts titled, "Character Education Quality Standards." This evaluation resource uses CEP's 11 principles. Each principle is stated and followed by sub-principles and bulleted descriptors. The scoring rubric is a scale from 0 to 4 representing poor implementation evidence to exemplary implementation. The booklet is free and can be obtained from CEP, 1025 Connecticut Ave., NW, Suite 1011, Washington, DC 20036; 800-988-8081, fax 202-296-7779.

The Character Education Partnership offers schools and school districts opportunities to apply for the National Schools of Character Awards. Each year, approximately 10 schools and school districts are recognized as models of effective character education.

After the initial screening, about 25 semifinalists are selected for a site visit by a two-person team. Following the visit, a panel selects award winners from the semifinalists list. Winners receive a flag for display and a $2000 check for program enhancement, and become part of a mentoring network. In addition, winners benefit from press releases, are featured in a yearly book on national schools of character, and are recognized at CEP national forum. CEP publishes a four-page flyer on how to apply for recognition.

The application guidelines can be obtained from CEP or downloaded from its web site www.character.org.

CEP also offers a Promising Practices Citation to school and school districts for implementing a unique and specific character education practice. It is an opportunity for schools and districts excelling in any one of what CEP calls "Eleven Principles of Effective Character Education." The one-page application flyer can be obtained from CEP or one may apply online using CEP's web site www.character.org or by email: geninfo@character.org or fax: 1-202-296-7779.

Center for the 4th & 5th Rs. "School as a Caring Community Profile" can be completed by staff, students (grades 4 and up), and parents. Cortland, N.Y.: State University of New York, Cortland. www.cortland.edu/www.c4n5rs.

Columbine Elementary School (Pre K-5), 175 Kelley St., Woodland Park, CO 80863. This character education award-winning school uses an instrument with a set of standards for personal and social responsibility that includes such skills as "practices organizational skills," "supports and interacts positively with others," "takes risks and accepts challenges," "accepts responsibility for behavior," and " listens attentively, follows directions, stays focused." Each skill is accompanied by a set of standard statements using the following scale: in progress, basic, proficient, and advanced.

DeRoche, E. & Williams, M. (2001). *Educating Hearts and Minds: A Comprehensive Character Education Framework*, 2nd edition, Thousand Oaks, Calif.: Corwin Press. Chapter 6, "Assessing Your Character Education Programs" includes a checklist of assessment standards, a character education effectiveness scale, school personnel's perceptions of the character education program, a school's problem inventory, students' misbehaviors and probable causes scale, a community involvement inventory, a questionnaire for assessing students views, student portfolios, a parent opinionnaire, and a classroom climate opinionnaire.

DeRoche, E. and Williams, M. (2001). *Character Education: A Guide for School Administrators*. Lanham, Maryland: Scarecrow Press. In chapter 9, you will find a criteria checklist for effective programs, program impact on students scale, questions for using outside evaluators, and questions for preparing evaluation reports.

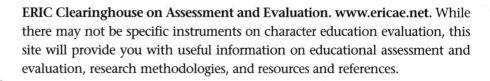

ERIC Clearinghouse on Assessment and Evaluation. www.ericae.net. While there may not be specific instruments on character education evaluation, this site will provide you with useful information on educational assessment and evaluation, research methodologies, and resources and references.

Fey, W. (1955). "Acceptance By Others and Its Relation to Acceptance of Self and Others: A Revaluation." *Journal of Abnormal and Social Psychology*, 30:274-276. "Acceptance of Others Scale" is provides 20 statements that tell how the respondent "deals with some feelings and attitudes about other people."

Fraser, B. (1989). *Assessing and Improving Classroom Environment*. Curtin University, Western Australia: Key Centre for School Science and Mathematics. Professor Fraser has authored three informative instruments that may be use by classroom teachers without charge. The first is "My Class Inventory," a 25-item yes/no scale that asks students to describe what their class is "actually like." The second instrument is called the "Constructivist Learning Environment Survey, "a 30-item scale asking students to respond to statements that reflect constructivist practices. A third instrument is a student questionnaire asking for a response on a 48-item list of statements about their teacher's behavior. Professor Fraser may be contacted at B. Fraser@smec.curtin.edu.au. His work is also referenced in an article by Walberg and Greenberg, (1997). "Using the Learning Environment Inventory." *Educational Leadership*, v54, n8, May, pp.45-47.

Gresham, F. and Elliott, S. *Social Skills Rating System (SSRS)*. The authors have designed a nationally standardized series of questionnaires that glean information on the social behaviors of children and adolescents from teachers, parents, and students themselves. It can be used in grades 3-12, with each questionnaire taking about 10-25 minutes to complete. SSRS screens students for problematic social behaviors and skills, and also assesses students whose problem behaviors and interpersonal skills are of concern.

American Guidance Service, 4201 Woodland Road, Circle Pines, MN 55014-1796. www.agsnet.com.

Howell, K. and Nolet, V. (2000). *Curriculum-Based Evaluation*. Note chapter 6, "Social Skills," and Appendix A.5, in which the authors provide a comprehensive list of social skills in the following categories: personal, interpersonal, problem solving, citizenship, classroom specific, and anger/violence. This skills list can be very helpful for designing evaluation instruments.

Kentfield School District (California) www.ksd.marin.k12.ca.us. This school district created two self-evaluation instruments that help students in their discussions with teachers (individually and in class) and parents delineate character traits that focus on the student as an individual, as a member of a group, and as a member of society. For example, the "Personal Character Development" instrument includes the traits of self-motivation, responsibility, empathy, trustworthiness, personal decision making,

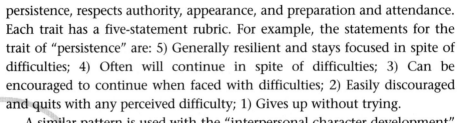

persistence, respects authority, appearance, and preparation and attendance. Each trait has a five-statement rubric. For example, the statements for the trait of "persistence" are: 5) Generally resilient and stays focused in spite of difficulties; 4) Often will continue in spite of difficulties; 3) Can be encouraged to continue when faced with difficulties; 2) Easily discouraged and quits with any perceived difficulty; 1) Gives up without trying.

A similar pattern is used with the "interpersonal character development" survey instrument. (From two presentations at the California Education Conference, 1999 & 2000).

Korpi, M. (n.d.). *Character Education Survey*. Three scales are available: student school climate scales, staff survey of school climate, and staff attitude survey about character education. To obtain this survey, email characteresearch@aol.com or visit www.characterresearch.org.

Leithwood, K., Aitken, R. and Jantzi, D. (2001) *Making Schools Smarter*. Thousand Oaks, Calif.: Corwin Press. The authors offer these useful evaluation survey instruments: school mission and goals, school policies and procedures, school-community partnerships, student participation and engagement-family educational culture, and district-community partnerships. For example, there is a 44-item school mission-and-goals survey seeking respondents' agreement or disagreement on eight factors: clarity, meaningfulness, awareness, use, currency, congruence, immediate focus, long-range focus (pp. 134-135).

Lewis, B. (1998). *What Do You Stand For? A Kid's Guide to Building Character*. Minneapolis: Free Spirit Publishing. Several reproducible instruments offered in this book include: character traits inventory, fears inventory, interest inventory, relationship inventory, learning styles inventory, honesty survey, integrity survey, tolerance survey, friendship survey , activism inventory, among others.

Loehrer, M.(1998). *How to Change a Rotten Attitude: A Manual for Building Character in Middle and High School Students*. Thousand Oaks, Calif.: Corwin Press. The author has developed and field-tested the LVAQ-Loehrer Virtue Assessment Questionnaire, a 26-item instrument based on the elements of two virtues—duty and desire.

Milson, A. *Teacher Efficacy and Character Education*. ERIC Clearinghouse on Assessment and Evaluation, 1129 Shriver Laboratory, College Park, MD 20742. Professor Milson has developed the Character Development Efficacy Belief Instrument, a 24-item instruments that asks elementary teachers to determine the extent to which they agree or disagree with a series of statements, such as "I find it difficult to persuade a student that respect for others is important." His findings suggest that most elementary teachers feel efficacious regarding most aspects of character education. How might teachers at your school respond to the items? (See SES 1.6.)

McMillan, J. (2001). *Classroom Assessment: Principles and Practice for Effective Instruction*. Boston: Allyn and Bacon. Of particular interest is chapter 10, "Assessing Affective Traits and Learning Targets."

National Association of Elementary School Principals. (2001). *Data-based Decision Making.* This is one volume in a five-volume set titled *Essentials for Principals* written by NAESP in cooperation with Educational Research Service. Included in this volume are such topics as ways to collect and use assessment data, the advantages of technology, and implementing a school-wide assessment program. Order from the National Principals Resource Center 800-386-2377 or online www.naesp.org.

Nebraska 4-H Youth Development. (n.d.) *Character Education Behavior Survey.* Lincoln, Neb.: University of Nebraska Cooperative Extension. This two-page questionnaire calls for teacher feedback about student behaviors prior to and after character education instruction.

North Carolina State Board of Education. (2002). *Character Education Informational Handbook and Guide.* Frye, M., et al (eds.). Raleigh, N.C.: Department of Public Instruction, Character Education Office. This excellent publication offers several sample assessment tools including a "school-site self-assessment" scale, "school as a caring community" survey and an example of a caring community scale used at a high school.

School Work Culture Profile. This instrument measures the extent of professional involvement in shaping the school's work culture, which is the relationships among the school's improvement plan, its staff development and instructional programs, and assessment processes. Contact Karolyn Synder, University of Southern Florida, 13604 Waterfall Way, Tampa FL 33624; 813-963-3899

School Climate Assessment Instruments. Go to www.character.org; click on "assessment" and you will find an index of instruments; click on "classroom/ school climate" for a listing of school and classroom climate evaluation instruments. The School Climate web page: www.westga.edu/~sclimate.

Scully, J. (2000). *The Power of Social Skills in Character Development: Helping Diverse Learners Succeed.* Port Chester, N.Y.: National Professional Resources, Inc. Throughout this book, the author provides several informal survey instruments, checklists, and questionnaires.

Vessels, G. (1998). *Character and Community Development: A School Planning and Teacher Training Handbook.* Westport, Conn.: Praeger Publishers. The author has created useful assessment instruments, including a classroom observation form, a school climate survey, classroom climate survey, and student character questionnaires for early and late elementary school years, and for middle and high school students.

Wagner, C. and Masden-Copas, P. (2002). "An Audit of the Culture Starts with Two Handy Tools." *Journal of Staff Development.* 23, 3: 42-53. It offers two handy tools in the article. The Self-Assessment: School Culture Triage is a 17-item survey for teachers and the instructional staff that includes a scoring guide, and the School Culture Audit includes an explanation of a five-step audit plan: 1) interviews, 2) observations, 3) survey with a 13-item instrument, 4) evaluation, and 5) presentation.

David Wangaard, the executive director of The School for Ethical Education, has designed a "Character Education Assessment Checklist." This checklist may be used as a self-assessment instrument for evaluating a current or new character education program. There are seven components in the instrument—mission, stake holders, environmental, program, staff, students, and parents. Each component has a series of statements and two scales, one for importance, the other for implementation. This eight-page instrument also has space for school-specific statements. Information about the instrument and its use can be obtained from the Character Development Group, P.O. Box 9211, Chapel Hill, NC 27515-9211; 919-967-2110; www.charactereducation.com.

READINGS

Bosworth, K. (1995). "Caring for Others and Being Cared For." *Phi Delta Kappan.* 26, 9: 686-693.

Bridges, L. (1995). *Assessment: Continuous Learning.* Portland, Me.: Stenhouse Publishers.

Burke, K. (1999). *The Mindful School: How to Assess Authentic Learning*, 3rd ed. Arlington Heights, Ill.: Skylight Professional Development.

Burnford, G., Fischer, J. and Hobson,D., eds. (2001). *Teachers Doing Research: The Power of Action Through Inquiry.* Rahwah, N.J.: Lawrence Erlbaum Publishers.

Dean, D. (1994). "How to Use Focus Groups." In *Handbook of Practical Program Evaluation.* Joseph S. Wholey, Harry P. Hatry, and Kathryn E. Newcomer, eds., San Francisco: Jossey-Bass Publishers.

DeRoche, E. & Williams, M. (2001). *Character Education: A Guide for School Administrators*, Lanham, Md.: Scarecrow Press.

DeRoche, E.(2000). "Leadership for Character Education Programs," *Journal of Humanistic Counseling, Education and Development*, 39, September: 41-46.

Dotson, A. & Wisont, K.(2001). *The Character Education Handbook: Establishing a Character Program in Your School.* Cleveland, Ohio: Character Press. Note chapter 10, "Measuring the Effect of Character Education."

Drummond, M. (1994). *Learning to See: Assessment Through Observation.* Portland, Me.: Stenhouse Publishers.

Educational Leadership, 56, 1 (September 1998)—the theme of this issue is "realizing a positive school climate."

Helms, E., Hunt, G. and Bedwell, L. (1999). "Meaningful instruction through understanding students values." *Middle School Journal*, 31, 1: 8-13.

Holcomb, E.. (1999). *Getting Excited About Data*. Thousand Oaks, Calif: Corwin Press. On pages 30-35, the author provides a valuable way to monitor your mission with a specific example and ideas for involving others in "walking the talk."

Hoffman, J. & Lee, A. (1997). *Character Education Workbook: For School Boards, Administrators, & Community Leaders*. Note the 4 Cs of leadership.

Huffman, H.A. (1994). *Developing a Character Education Program: One School District's Experience*. Alexandria, Va.: Association for Supervision and Curriculum Development.

Lashway, L. "Data Analysis for School Improvement." *Research Roundup*. 19, 2, (Winter 2002-2003). Alexandria, Va.: National Association of Elementary School Principals.

Lo, Y. and Cartledge, G. "Using Office Referral Data to Improve School Discipline," *Streamlined Seminar*, 20, 2 (Winter 2002). Alexandria, Va.: National Association of Elementary School Principals.

Logan, K. (1997). *Getting the Schools You Want: A Step-by-Step Guide to Conducting Your Own Curriculum Management Audit*. Thousand Oaks, Calif.: Corwin Press.

Morgan, N. and Saxton, J. (1996). *Asking Better Questions: Models, Techniques, and Activities for Engaging Students in Learning*. Portland, Me.: Stenhouse Publishers.

Murphy, M. (1998). *Character Education in America's Blue Ribbon Schools*. Lancaster, PA: Technomic Publishing Co. Note chapter 9, "Evaluating the effectiveness of character education in the blue ribbon schools."

Power, B. (1996). *Taking Note: Improving Your Observational Notetaking*. Portland, Me.: Stenhouse Publishers.

Roberts, W. and Morotti, A. "What Is Your School's Mental Health Profile? *NASSP Bulletin*, 85, 622 (2001): 59-68.

Patten, M.(2000). *Understanding Research Methods: An Overview of the Essentials*, 2nd ed. Los Angeles: Pyrczak Publishing.

Sergiovani, T. (1992). *Moral Leadership: Getting to the Heart of School Improvement*. San Francisco: Jossey-Bass Publishers.

Service Learning: Linking Classroom and Communities. (1999) California Department of Education, CDE Press, Sales Office, P.O. Box 271, Sacramento, CA 95812-0271

Schaps, E. "Building Community in School." *Principal*, 76, 2 (November 1996): 29-31.

Swick, K. et. al. (nd). *Service Learning and Character Education: Walking the Talk.* Learn and Serve America Program, Department of Service Learning, 1201 New York Ave., NW, Washington, D.C. 20525 www.nationalservice.org.

The Commission for Ethical and Responsible Student Behavior. (2001). *Taking Responsibility.* Augusta: Maine Department of Education. The State of Maine has established standards for ethical and responsible behavior in schools focusing on the core values of respect, honesty, compassion, fairness, responsibility, and courage. Each core value is defined with the preface "An ethical person is...." As an example for the core value "courage," the statement reads: "The ethical person is courageous in the face of ethical challenges." (p. 31)

Veale, J., Morley, R. and Erickson, C. (2002). *Practical Evaluation for Collaborative Services.* Thousand Oaks, Calif.: Corwin Press.